FARRAR
STRAUS
GIROUX

S T R I V I N G

T O W A R D S

B E I N G

The Letters of Thomas Merton

and Czeslaw Milosz

STRIVING

TOWARDS

BEING

The Letters of Thomas Merton
and Czeslaw Milosz

EDITED BY

ROBERT FAGGEN

Farrar, Straus and Giroux
New York

Designed by Debbie Glasserman
First edition, 1997

Library of Congress Cataloging-in-Publication Data
Merton, Thomas, 1915–1968.
    Striving towards being : the letters of Thomas Merton and Czeslaw
Milosz / edited by Robert Faggen.
        p. cm.
    ISBN 0-374-27100-3 (alk. paper)
    1. Merton, Thomas, 1915–1968—Correspondence. 2. Miłosz, Czesław—
Correspondence. 3. Trappists—United States—Correspondence.
4. Monks—United States—Correspondence. 5. Authors, Polish—20th
century— I. Miłosz, Czesław. II. Faggen, Robert. III. Title.
BX4705.M4884A4 1996
271'.12502—dc20   96-23827
                                                                            CIP

INTRODUCTION

The decade-long correspondence (1958 to 1968) of Thomas Merton and Czeslaw Milosz represents a mutually edifying dialogue, a *concerto grosso*, between two powerful voices seeking to maintain faith in some of the most turbulent years of the late twentieth century. They recognized totalitarianism, scientism, atomic war, and racism as among the greatest threats to mankind's ability to sustain belief in a just God and in Providence. Beyond observations about the twentieth century, the letters reveal significant differences between the experience of two Christians, one an American Trappist monk born in France (1915) and the other a Lithuanian-born (1911) Polish poet living in self-exile in Montgeron, a small town outside Paris, and then in the United States in Berkeley. Both writers lived in solitude, and the letters reflect their sense of the desirability of that solitude, as reaction and protest to the political and social absurdities around them. But both also explore the inadequacy of a life of solitude as an answer to the most pressing questions of faith. Merton's solitude was the self-imposed isolation of a monk in the increasingly tumultuous world of post-war America, and Milosz's the more forced isolation of an émigré who found himself unable to tolerate the evils of Stalinist Poland. In addition to being cut off from any significant Polish-speaking audience, Milosz found the Paris of the 1950s dominated by intellectuals and artists—Sartre and Picasso, among others—sympathetic to Stalinism and Communist revolution. Both men were poets who valued literature as a way to revelation. And though Merton knew no Polish and though English was a third language for Milosz, their correspondence is a clear and vibrant testament to the intensity and profundity of their friendship. They met only twice, first when Milosz visited Merton in the Abbey of Gethsemani in Louisville, Kentucky, in September 1964 and then when Merton stopped in Berkeley, where Milosz was teaching, in October 1968. But their letters reveal a powerful relationship of mutual spiritual guidance.

Merton initiated the correspondence in 1959 after reading Milosz's study of the social psychology of Communism, *The Captive Mind.* Unknown in the West for his poetry, Milosz found a receptive audience in a post-war America eager to understand the lure and dangers of Communism. In Merton, Milosz had found a more subtle audience, one which recognized that the book was not simply a condemnation of Communism but an attempt to understand the lure of Marxism in the wake of the erosion of the religious imagination. Milosz's aim was to liberate the mind from the captive thought that attempted to satisfy the human need for faith in a true God; it was not merely a piece of anti-Soviet political propaganda.

Milosz's eager response to Merton reveals his need for a spiritual father, one who could lead him out of the bottle of his own egotism and his growing view that the world, following old Manichaean heresies and influenced by the writings of Simone Weil, was ruled by an evil demiurge. What becomes clear is that Milosz admired and even sought the life of contemplation and solitude but also feared that there could be no way out of the struggle of the world and no way out of the trap of the self. Born and raised a Catholic, Milosz, as an observer of nature, a student of science, and a survivor of the Nazi occupation of Warsaw and the Stalinist regime in Poland, had grave doubts about the value of literature and poetry in relation to salvation. Committed to the sensuous world of art but aware of its meaninglessness when only an exercise in form detached from the contemplation of God, Milosz thought that Merton, a deeply religious man who did not see literature and poetry at odds with faith, could provide a vision of religious experience translatable into images on the borderland between art and religion, poetry and theology.

Milosz had had spiritual guides before, and they appear in the correspondence. His older cousin, the French poet

O. V. de L. Milosz, whose symbolic and mystical vision had prefigured Einstein's eradication of the soul-crushing concepts of absolute space and time, had mentored and supported the young poet and deeply influenced his sense of the poetic vocation. Another important figure was Albert Einstein himself. While working in the United States as an attaché for the Polish government in the late 1940s, Milosz sought out Einstein's advice on whether or not he should break with his country and emigrate. Einstein told him that as a poet it was crucial that he stay with his native audience. He also believed that humanity was inherently good, and that the situation in Poland would change soon. Milosz has recounted the meeting at some length in his autobiographical *Native Realm: A Search for Self-definition* (1968), describing how he had thought of Einstein as a spiritual father but that the revelation of Einstein's political optimism had made him impishly skeptical. Some of Milosz's best poetry—notably "To Robinson Jeffers" and "To Raja Rao"—describes dialogues with writers and thinkers to whose spirituality and vision he is deeply attracted but who cannot quite assuage his greatest doubts.

Milosz's letters to Merton represent another such "poem." Though he at first approached Merton as a mentor, Milosz appears to take on that role himself as the correspondence develops. Milosz does not hesitate to confess his own failings and to take issue with Merton's views or his writings for falling short of his expectations. Those expectations were extraordinarily high, as Milosz was seeking no less than a new cosmology that would illuminate the contradictions he saw between the God of the Hebrew Bible and the God of the New Testament and provide a justification of the Christian anthropocentric vision in the modern world. And neither William James's epiphenomena of religious experience nor Teilhard de Chardin's attempts to wed biology and theology would do. Milosz was critical of Merton on two major points. He felt that Merton was insufficiently skeptical of pantheism and the tendency to see nature as beneficent or a source of divine revelation. And he was skeptical of Merton's pacifism and political activism. A deep distrust of the stance of moral purity in an evil world kept Milosz from denouncing the necessity of war or the use of atomic weapons, though he certainly does not portray himself as a hawk. The letters reveal the extent to which Milosz feared the impact of vulgarized nihilism and Marxism, which he witnessed as a professor at Berkeley in the early 1960s, particularly for the way it would make America ripe for an equally dangerous right-wing reaction.

Merton held fast to his defense of pacifism against the orders of the Church that he keep silent. His letter of March 21, 1962, to Milosz became number 56 of the over one hundred letters he wrote within a year against nuclear proliferation and distributed secretly in mimeographed packets as his *Cold War Letters*. Despite his life as a Trappist monk, Merton remained "a lone wolf" within the Catholic Church. Merton shared Milosz's distrust of the political authority of the Church and sought ways to circumvent it. Milosz proposed ways in which Merton could become a spiritual leader in the United States, even going so far as to suggest using mass media to help the nation out of some of its mediocrity. We learn a great deal about Milosz's reaction to life in the United States, the differences between the role of Catholicism in Eastern Europe and in America, the troubled state of his own faith, and many of the struggles which were generating some of his most important poetry and prose. The letters reveal the soul of a man for whom exile had become the necessary condition of anyone in honest pursuit of the real.

Deeply interested in the problems of confession and in the possibilities of spiritual autobiography, Milosz was inspired by Merton's powerful *The Sign of Jonas*, which he read while working on *Native Realm* and certainly had in mind years later when writing his own spiritual diary, *The Year of the Hunter*. And the letters reveal how much Milosz became an influence and spiritual guide for Merton as he sought a realm of "integrity" beyond protest, beyond acceptance of life's absurdity, and beyond the practices of religion. Milosz insisted on the necessity of always "striving towards being," and Merton found himself inspired by Milosz's urging. David Belcastro has pointed to the impact Milosz had on Merton's essay "Notes for a Philosophy of Solitude"* and, most important, on Merton's reading of Camus, which resulted in seven essays written from 1966 to 1968 (included in *The Literary Essays* of Thomas Merton, 1981). Camus, Milosz's friend and a fellow devotee of Simone Weil, became a major focal point of Merton's attempt to find a universal ground for faith in a world whose moral predicament made estrangement a viable but precarious path. Guided by Milosz, Merton saw the vocation of solitude as leading to that "emptiness" in which one "does not find points upon which to base a contrast between himself and others,"† a nothingness in which all being and all love begin. Years later, we still find Milosz seeking that being in the *sunyata*, the "nothingness" of Buddhism, a universal ground of being where Eastern and Western religious traditions can meet.‡ While Milosz's interest in Eastern thought began with his readings in Schopenhauer, it was no doubt

*David Belcastro, "Czeslaw Milosz's Influence on Thomas Merton's 'Notes for a Philosophy of Solitude,' " *The Merton Annual* 7:1(1994), pp. 21–32. Merton, "Notes for a Philosophy of Solitude," in *Disputed Questions*, 1960, pp. 179–94.

†Merton, "Notes for a Philosophy of Solitude," p. 187.

‡Milosz's "Dialogue on Buddhism," published in *Znak* in 1995, discussing the concept of the universal *sunyata* in Keiji Nishitani's *Religion and Nothingness*, 1982, and Christian writers, including Merton, who embraced Buddhism.

fueled by his dialogue with Merton. Thus the correspondence, which ended with Merton's death in 1968, played a crucial role in both men's lives as they struggled against mere protest and existential solitude and toward the possibilities of universal faith and love. Written in a spirit of rare understanding and fellowship, the letters reveal a great deal about the hearts and minds of their authors and also about some of the most important spiritual questions which have challenged mankind in the late twentieth century.

Robert Faggen
Claremont McKenna College
Fall 1996

STRIVING

TOWARDS

BEING

The Letters of Thomas Merton

and Czeslaw Milosz

Our Lady of Gethsemani   Dec. 6, 1958
Trappist, Kentucky

Dear Mr Milosz:

Having read your remarkable book "The Captive
Mind"* I find it necessary to write to you, as without your
help I am unable to pursue certain lines of thought which
this book suggests. I would like to ask you a couple of questions and hope you will forgive this intrusion.

First of all I would like to say that I found your book to
be one of the most intelligent and stimulating it has been
my good fortune to read for a very long time. It is an important book, which makes most other books on the present
state of man look abjectly foolish. I find it especially important for myself in my position as a monk, a priest and a
writer. It is obvious that a Catholic writer in such a time as
ours has an absolute duty to confine himself to reality and
not waste his time in verbiage and empty rationalisations.
Unfortunately, as I have no need to point out to you, most
of us do this and much worse. The lamentable, pitiable emptiness of so much Catholic writing, including much of my
own, is only too evident. Your book has come to me, then,
as something I can call frankly "spiritual", that is to say as
the inspiration of much thought, meditation and prayer

*Milosz's *The Captive Mind* appeared in English in 1953, translated by Jane Zie-
lonko.

about my own obligations to the rest of the human race, and about the predicament of us all.

It seems to me that, as you point out, and as other writers like yourself say or imply (Koestler,* Camus etc) there *has to be* a third position, a position of integrity, which refuses subjection to the pressures of the two massive groups ranged against each other in the world. It is quite simply obvious that the future, in plain dialectical terms, rests with those of us who risk our heads and our necks and everything in the difficult, fantastic job of finding out the new position, the ever changing and moving "line" that is no line at all because it cannot be traced out by political dogmatists. And that is the difficulty, and the challenge. I am the last in the world to pretend to know anything about it. One thing I do know, is that anyone who is interested in God Who is Truth, has to break out of the ready-made shells of the "captive" positions that offer their convenient escapes from freedom—one who loves freedom must go through the painful experience of seeking it, perhaps without success. And for my part, this letter represents a hearty peek at the inside of my own particular kind of shell, the nature and hardness of which I leave you to imagine.

*Arthur Koestler (1905–83), German anthropologist, social critic, and psychologist, author of novels and essays, including *Darkness at Noon* (1941) and "The Initiates," in *The God That Failed: Six Studies in Communism,* edited by R.H.S. Crossman (1950).

First of all, I would like to get other books of yours, whether in English or in French. Or articles, anything that can help me. Tell me the names of some books, I can order them. Send me copies of articles if you have them. In exchange I will be honored to let you have any books of mine you might want.

Then, I am interested in Alpha and Beta*—who are they, what are their books, and are these books available in French or English?

I would also like to know who are Gamma and Delta, naturally.†

Is there anything I can do for you? It seems to me that the most obvious thing I can give you is the deep and friendly interest of a kindred mind and a will disposed for receptiveness and collaboration. And of course, my prayers. The address from which I write to you is that of a Cistercian

*Alpha and Beta are the allegorical names Milosz gave two of the four individuals he portrayed in *The Captive Mind.* "Alpha, the Moralist" was Jerzy Andrzejewski (1909–83), a Polish novelist, author of *Ashes and Diamonds.* "Beta, the Disappointed Lover" was Tadeusz Borowski (1922–51), author of *This Way to the Gas, Ladies and Gentlemen,* a sardonic depiction of concentration-camp existence. Borowski survived Auschwitz but later committed suicide, placing his head in an oven.

†"Gamma, the Slave of History" was Jerzy Putrament (1910–), one of the members of the literary group founded by Milosz known as "Zagary." He was the author of two volumes of poetry before the war, *Yesterday the Return* (1935) and *Forest Road* (1938), but became involved with the Polish Communist Army and the Polish press in the Soviet Union sponsored by the Communist Union of Patriots. "Delta, the Troubadour" was Konstanti Galczynski (1905–53), author of *The End of the World: Visions of St. Idlefonse, or a Satire on the Universe* (1929), an apocalyptic work in the guise of opera buffa.

monastery, where I have lived and worked for seventeen years as a monk and a priest. If you ever come by this way, I would be eager to have a talk with you and glad to welcome you to this house. I presume, however, you still live in France. You may reply to me in French or English, as you prefer.

Faithfully yours in Christ
Thomas Merton

✺

Czeslaw Milosz   Jan. 17, 1959
10, avenue de la Grange
Montgeron (Seine et Oise)
France

Dear Mr. Merton,

Your letter travelled quite a long time. I thank you cordially for it and feel it created already a tie between us. In the last few years I have been writing mostly for the Polish public and publishing in my native tongue, many new problems, polemics etc. so *The Captive Mind*, written in 1951, got so to say submerged in my consciousness by other elements. That book was written in extremis by a poet who could not address foreign language readers in verse and hesitated between two aims: to convey the meaning of the

"Eastern" experience to those not acquainted with it, to tell the truth to his colleagues in Poland. *The Captive Mind* has been exerting a considerable influence over there since its appearance in Polish, in Paris, 1953. Many times I asked visitors from Poland: after all, why are you impressed by that book? What I say everybody knows. They answered: yes, but to know and to read about what one knows is not the same. The spell was broken in Poland in 1956 or rather was breaking down gradually in 1955–1956. Now I have friendly relations with a majority of my confrères over there and respect them as they are in a more difficult situation than I. Consider my moral scruples: it is not easy to write a pamphlet against living human beings and how can one be severe without usurping for himself the place of a judge? You ask me about Alpha, Beta, Gamma, Delta. For Alpha my chapter on him was a blow and perhaps contributed to his change. He changed completely. And he does not keep a grudge. On the contrary, we are again friends—at distance, as he, contrary to many others, does not make trips abroad. I shall try to find for you one of his books published in French translation. Beta committed suicide and is considered today one of the "victims of Stalinism". For Gamma my book and my person are obsession, he hates me and ascribes to my influence hostility of other writers by which he is surrounded now in Poland. As to Delta, he died in 1953 and his collected works are highly appreciated. To complete the image I should perhaps advise you to read *The Broken Mirror*, a collection of writings from contemporary Poland, edited by Pawel Mayewski, introduction by Lionel Trilling. Of course, Poland is by no means typical, that is quite an exceptional case and, unfortunately, my description in *The Captive Mind* stands for other Central-Eastern European countries. And I disagree with what Lionel Trilling says in his preface to the volume.

I went through much despair. I was helped in my despair by things and some human beings—among others by Simone Weil, through her writings. I felt afterwards she could help not only me and succeeded in publishing her *Chosen Writings* in my Polish translation*—a book of 350 pages. It seems, judging by letters from Poland, that the book is useful, it clarifies certain issues, especially in a country where there is a continual tug of war between the clergy and the Marxists (I do not mention the authorities, their intellectual influence is now small). I do not know how to initiate you in a few sentences into problems of a writer who is separated from the Western public by a barrier of language. Not only I do not attempt to translate my poetry but I am unable to write prose in any other tongue than my own. I suspect a

---

*Simone Weil (1909–43), French philosopher and mystic whose work influenced T. S. Eliot, Samuel Beckett, Camus, and Milosz, among many others. Her works include *Oppression and Liberty, Waiting for God,* "The Iliad or the Poem of Force." Weil was critical of the Marxist notion of "dialectical materialism" as a contradiction in terms.

sort of psychological obstacle or a tendency to self-protection. The result is that several essays of mine are available to those who read Polish only. To look for translators is such a tedious task. Besides, there is a resistance against accepting a role which is not my own, pretending I am a Western writer while I am not. I like Camus but feel we belong to different worlds. The trouble is that when jumping from one circle of experience (collective experience) into the other one has to explain too much. This is an excellent discipline but often one prefers short-cuts and allusions. You mention a third way, you rightly say it should be invented. Why, the whole of literary Paris proclaims it every day but their search, with one or two exceptions, is not genuine. I live in a little town near Paris and look at that literary turmoil with a dose of scorn—do not accuse me of pride as this is not my individual pride, I share it with young writers from Poland who visit me here, perhaps we all are more mature—at a price.

I suppose there are no solutions, they should be improvised and if Negroes from Martinique or Guadeloupe with whom I like to talk in Paris conceive everything in terms of their poor islands, they are right. Before being universal one has to be particular and so it is with my half-chosen limit of one tongue, with my "engagement" in changing things of Poland. How to combine "transcendence" and "devenir" has been always my main question. I contribute here in Paris to a monthly, *Kultura*, a kind of miracle of obstinacy, appearing regularly for 12 years, in spite of constant financial troubles, and having devoted readers in Poland. The West does not help enterprises of that type. As to millions of dollars thrown every year through the window for "combatting communism" I have my own opinion on that subject which you can guess from *The Captive Mind*.

It happened that at the same time as your letter I received last issues of some Catholic monthlies published in Poland (they are on a very good level). In one I find fragments from your book *No Man Is an Island* (from the chapter on vocation), in another your *Meditation in Solitude*.* In general I see often translations from your works in periodicals and I hope you forgive editors who have some difficulties in their contacts with people abroad. I confess I do not know your prose books, from time to time I meet your poetry. A few years ago I translated one of your poems—for an issue of *Kultura* dedicated to American literature (there were poems by Wallace Stevens, Carlos Williams, Ransom,† Merton). I would be glad to receive those books of yours which you like, in poetry or prose.

A great lacuna in *The Captive Mind* is, it seems to me,

---

*Milosz refers to a selection translated by M. Mortstin-Gorska in *Znak* 1960: 1–5, 7–8, 10–11, as well as a fragment from *Meditatio pauperis in solitudine*, translated by E. Misiolek, in *Wiez* 1958: 8.

†John Crowe Ransom (1888–1974), poet, founder of the *Kenyon Review*.

lack of a chapter on the Church. In a way I can be pardoned, in view of the extreme complexity of the subject and my shyness (I have always been crypto-religious and in a conflict with the political aspect of Polish Catholicism, which is perhaps similar to Irish Catholicism). Nevertheless, my book can create a wrong impression in such attentive readers as you. Poland is the only country of the Soviet bloc where, besides magical beliefs of masses and the clergy of not high intellectual level, there is a vigorous Catholic thought, lively interest for philosophical and theological problems, everything is permeated by that religious atmosphere which cannot be found in Czechoslovakia or Germany or Russia. So the impact of Marxist philosophy proved too weak to overcome it. If you want to know my opinion on *The Captive Mind*, I judge it as a book of simplification (perhaps unavoidable), as a political pamphlet belonging to the sphere of action, when we throw something on the balance. Can we act without committing a sin? Not that I intended to simplify. But when you shape the material, when you have to eliminate and passion guides you—you succumb to the pesanteur of the very process. In fact I love those people against whom I directed my anger much more than I show. I did not succeed in showing my love and my whole thought. How well I know that shame which comes from (perhaps unavoidable) elimination, from fear of being too complicated, too unaccessible, from your own rigidity. That is why your letter renewed all my pangs of conscience.

It seems to me that communist experience in Poland made inner life of human beings more intense and that the young generation is better than before the war. Of course the situation in the years 1949–1955 was unbearable and can become unbearable from one day to the other. Yet, if we measure systems by inner search, by intellectual openness, the evil produced good results. Yes, had not occurred that change in 1956, I would be pessimistic, this is obvious.

In foreign languages I have published besides *The Captive Mind* two books. One novel, *The Seizure of Power*, describes events in Poland in 1944; it was published in New York by Criterion Books but I do not think you can find it, so I can send you it in French. I do not like novels. They are inferior to other literary kinds. I am rather fond of my novel which appeared in French as *Sur les bords de l'Issa** and in German as *Tal der Issa*. Fortunately, it has nothing political, describes my native countryside (I was born in Lithuania) and is centered on the problem of death in Nature (hunting, rites of magic etc.). But, written in an idiom, does not go well with the French language. Do you read the German?

I profit from the occasion to ask you whether you know

---

* *The Issa Valley*, translated by Louis Iribarne, 1978.

the works of Oscar de L. Milosz. He was a relative of mine and a French poet (died in 1939). I am sure that discovery would give you much. New edition of his complete work is being published now in Paris. His *Miguel Manara* is an ideal play to be staged in monasteries (story of Don Juan and his conversion)—though it was played the last year with success for lay public in Paris. Also his poems, the novel *Amoureuse Initiation*,* and his metaphysical treatises, *Ars Magna* and *Les Arcanes*. He was a great poet, superior (and not only in my opinion) to Claudel.† Your library should acquire his works. I do not like Claudel.

You kindly ask me what you can do for me. Perhaps you know a good and honest literary agent in New York. I have never had one and it is time to do something in this respect.

I thank you for your warm and brotherly letter. It was a joy for me to receive it.

Czeslaw Milosz

P.S. My road is and was more torturous than it seems from this letter. Forgive me its external, informative character.

*A volume of O. V. de L. Milosz's works is available in English: *The Noble Traveler: The Life and Writings of O. V. de L. Milosz*, selected and edited by Christopher Bamford, with an introduction by Czeslaw Milosz, 1985. *Amorous Initiation: A Novel of Sacred and Profane Love* was translated by Belle N. Burke, 1994; first published as *L'Amoureuse Initiation* in Paris in 1910.

†Paul Claudel (1868–1955), poet, playwright, and essayist renowned for his lyric poems *Cinq grandes odes* (1910). He converted to Catholicism and entered a monastery in 1900.

There is a Japanese film *Rashomon*, where 4 subjective versions of one event are given. I practice *Rashomon* too much so I am sometimes afraid of that delectatio morosa.

※

My Dear Milosz:

Thanks for your splendid letter. It was delayed in reaching me by the inevitable monastic barriers and also by the annual retreat. And I have been thinking about it for a week or so. The books you said you might send have not yet arrived, but there again there are many delays. I look forward very eagerly to reading anything of yours, anything by Alpha. My German however is slow, so I cannot afford the time to read a book in German unless there is no other way of getting at it. I am sure I will enjoy *Sur les bords de l'Issa*. The few passages on Lithuania in the *Captive Mind* were striking and delightful.

I am sorry that I did not think more deeply about the trouble of heart I might cause you in writing so bluntly and glibly about the *Captive Mind*. Obviously I should have realized the many problems that would be involved. Like all the people here I have I suppose a sort of fantastic idea of the Iron Curtain—as if people on either side of it were simply dead to each other. The abyss between Abraham's bosom and Dives in hell. From what you write in the book, Alpha would certainly react as you have said. I have a great esteem for him and shall keep him in my prayers. And I can't say I am fond of Gamma. A real Stalinist type. Beta is perhaps something new to me, and Delta is familiar. I shall certainly get hold of the *Broken Mirror*. Trilling I generally take with a grain of salt (I knew him at Columbia where he was a professor).

Whatever you may feel about the *Captive Mind* (and I will not presume to try to make you feel otherwise) it is certainly a book that had to be written and evidently such a book could not be written at all unless it were written with terrible shortcomings. All were necessary, perhaps. Good will come of the suffering involved for you and for others. It is an exceptional book, in my opinion. It is one of the very few books about the writer and Communism, or about Communism itself, that has any real value as far as I can see. The rest are often just compilations of magic formulas and exorcisms, or plain platitudes. I agree with you with all my heart in feeling revulsion at the standard, superficial attitude taken by "the west" on the common, political and social level, to Russia etc. Revulsion in fact at the hypocrisy on both sides. *No one* giving a thought to human values and persons, to man's spirit, to his real destiny, to his real obligation to rebuild his world from the ground up, on the ruins of what past generations have left him. I mean no one except those who are in the middle, and who realize that they are caught between the two millstones. All the others, just helping the stones to grind, for the sake of grinding. But precisely as you say, those who are ground are coming out as clean flour.

Under separate cover I am sending you a manuscript which might be of interest to *Kultura* and which says something about the intellectual caught between tyrannies. It is called a "Letter to an Innocent Bystander" and you will get it eventually by ordinary mail. I tell you in all earnestness that it is a deep need for me to at least make some kind of gesture of participation in a work like that done by *Kultura*, to try to offer something of mine that might apply to the situation. I am very happy whenever I hear of a Catholic review in Poland printing something of mine, but I feel that the things they have used are to a great extent beside the point, though that may not be true. In any case it is unbearable to me to feel that I may have let myself get too far away from the actual problems of my time in a kind of pious detachment that is an indefensible luxury. There are all sorts of complicated angles to this, though. There is something much too mental and abstract, something too parochial about a great deal of Catholic thought and Catholic spirituality today, and this applies to the contemplatives in large measure. So much of it is all in the head. And in politics it is even worse: all the formulas, the gestures, the animosities, and the narrowness. I can easily understand your attitude though I do not know the situation. I can understand your looking for something in Simone Weil and am glad you translated her. Personally I found a great deal that rang a bell for me in *Dr Zhivago* and I very much like Berdyaev. There are people in the Orthodox Theological Institute (Institut Saint Serge) in Paris who are doing some tremendous thinking in spiritual things (Evdokimov for instance). Do you happen to be able to look up the address of that place? I would be grateful if you could find it, for instance in the phone book, and let me know. I might want to write to them some day. Among the Catholics, Bouyer is writing some good things, also of course De Lubac, Daniélou* etc. And then there is Guardini, who is splendid. I have never been able to read a line of Claudel's big fat poems, but I like *Jeanne d'Arc au bucher* and some of his prose, particularly about Japan. Japan is another obsession of mine. Not Rashomon—yet! Only Zen.

Who are the Martiniquais you know? Césaire and Glissant? I like their work very much, though I have had a hard time getting hold of anything by Césaire. Salute them for me!

About your poetry in English—this thought occurred to me, it may be a bad one, but it just passed through my head:

*Jean Daniélou (1905–74), French theologian and philosopher, author of *Dieu et Nous* (*God and the Ways of Knowing*), 1954.

why not just write out an English version of two or three short ones that you like, any kind of version, and let me try to use my ingenuity and guesswork and polish them up into versions which you could then check. This may be a crazy scheme and may not even be honest, I don't know. But to me it seems possible—at least something we might try, but of course since I know absolutely no Polish . . .

I thought of mentioning your work to Victoria Ocampo,* editor of *Sur* in Buenos Aires. There must be someone down there who can translate from Polish—*Sur* would be delighted to get something by you. I will tell Victoria to write to you, as I intend to write her soon. She writes perfect French. She might want to run a Polish number of *Sur* and that would be a splendid thing. I am sure she will jump at the idea.

The main question you ask—about an agent. My agent is very good and she would certainly be delighted to help you out. She is Naomi Burton, of Curtis Brown Ltd. Curtis Brown is represented in Paris by Hoffman who is a very tough cookie. I do not deal with him directly. But Naomi in New York is very nice and very efficient. I highly recommend her,

*Victoria Ocampo (1891–1979), Argentinian writer, editor, and publisher. *Testimonios*, her ten volumes of essays, was published 1935–37. She was founder and director of *Sur*, a literary review that published writers as prominent and diverse as Thomas Mann, Henry Miller, Martin Heidegger, Simone Weil, Merton, and Camus. Merton letters to Ocampo are included in Thomas Merton, *The Courage for Truth: Letters to Writers*, edited by Christine M. Bochen.

we are very good friends and I will mention you to her when I next write. Hoffman of course is highly efficient.

I shall certainly look up Oscar de L. Milosz, who sounds very interesting. I had heard the name but no more.

Of my own work, I am sending you two packets: one of small things, *Prometheus*, *Monastic Peace*, and the *Tears of the Blind Lions*. Then a full length book *The Sign of Jonas* and another less long, *Thoughts in Solitude* though I fear perhaps the latter may seem to you esoteric and sterile. It is a book about which I am quite divided. It is based on notes about things to which I personally attach some importance, but these notes were revised and dressed up by me and became what I take to be a little commercial and hence false. I don't know if this is scrupulosity. The book in any case is by no means adequate. I should be interested to know very frankly if it bores you completely and seems to you to be completely alien, bourgeois etc. That would be worth knowing. The poems alas are not too good. If there is any other book of mine you hear of that you would like, I will gladly send it. Or anything I can get for you, I will send.

Milosz—life is on our side. The silence and the Cross of which we know are forces that cannot be defeated. In silence and suffering, in the heartbreaking effort to be honest in the midst of dishonesty (most of all our *own* dishonesty), in all these is victory. It is Christ in us who drives us through darkness to a light of which we have no conception and which can only be found by passing through apparent despair. Everything has to be tested. All relationships have to be tried. All loyalties have to pass through fire. Much has to be lost. Much in us has to be killed, even much that is best in us. But Victory is certain. The Resurrection is the only light, and with that light there is no error.

> Deep affection and solidarity in Christ—
> Tom Merton

❋

Feb 28, 1959

Dear Milosz:

I realize it might seem a great impertinence to offer this* as reading for people behind the Iron Curtain, and when I wrote to you about it in my last letter I had not considered that fact. However, if it is understood that it was written for other intellectuals on *this side* of the curtain, it might not seem so inappropriate. But I should never presume to speak up, in my safe corner of the world, and try to tell people in grave danger how to be "honest". God forbid. You can use your discretion in this matter and if it is simply useless, then

*"Letter to an Innocent Bystander."

please return it. And tell me if it is really a piece of pre-sumptuous complacency. I have no way of getting a real perspective otherwise.

Faithfully,
Tom Merton

※

Before May 21, 1959
Easter Saturday

Dear Merton,

You seem to give me credit of wisdom. In fact I am un-easy about being an adult and standing alone, that's why I was always looking for masters and teachers as if by a lack of confidence in myself. My independence has been so to say enforced upon me by circumstances. Your essay I con-sider of great usefulness and actuality for both sides. The problem of "us" and "them" is especially actual at this mo-ment as the Union of Writers in Poland is under a violent attack—writers fight a hopeless battle against censorship and the Party's demands. I shall translate your essay and it will be published soon in *Kultura*. I do not know how to render the title—"bystander" is untranslatable, there is only a word meaning "temoin". Is your essay being published, or was it published in English? Should I give a note of explanatory character—not on your name, as you are known to Polish reading public, but perhaps you have some wishes.

The trouble with "them" is, as I know from my experience, that they leave us a very narrow margin. In America one is pushed into a position of "innocent bystander", in Europe pressures are different. It has been my problem for years—a game with "them" with full awareness what is at stake but also with awareness that a compromise is a maximum which can be achieved: they believe that they fool us, we believe that we fool them. After all I was for 5 years an official of the Embassy in Washington. But before the war it was even worse, since then I was not active, lost, and convinced that nothing could be done, just waiting for the inevitable. My experiences in Paris, after I broke with the Polish government in 1951, were also far from sweet. In this connection I should confess that I do not understand the notion of Providence and am very much on the side of Simone Weil who preferred to leave as much as possible to necessity ruling the world. I do not know whether by using the highest name we do not commit an act against piety. In any case I still wonder that I survived. "They" on this side use of course refugees as their tools in the struggle of "anticommunism". What can be told about those matters is terrifying. Of course there are various levels, starting with poor fellows in a nightmarish camp Valka near Nurnberg. But writers also have to pay a price and, with very rare exceptions, they eat only if they "work in anti-communism", poor slaves of their fear, no more free than their brothers in communist countries. For *The Captive Mind* I have been denounced to the police: "not enough" anti-communist and probably an agent; while hideous smell in Paris literary circles: a bourgeois, he writes against what is sacrosanct. I cannot say that I resolved the problem and if I live, with wife and two children, it is only thanks to what I can call miracles and a spirit of légereté, something learned and not innate. But the frontier between them and us is hazy. Example, Camus and pressures to which he was subjected by all the "bien pensants" of the Left Bank and extremely vicious leftist literary press able to kill through cruel jokes. The issue was Algeria—we think probably the same on this subject but we are foreigners and not natives of Algeria ("poor whites") as Camus is. That was a kind of trap and he reacted, I feel, in a wrong, perhaps, way, as we, resisting pressures, are sometimes tempted by our pride. The trouble is that any action, also an action against those who yield power, becomes, through the very nature of action, a group action and we have to accept to be ranged together with people whom we dislike. Etiquettes are being glued to us ("communist", "anti-communist", "catholic" etc) and to a certain extent there is no help. Pride or ambition sometimes mislead us when we want to be individuals and not just members of a given group. But in general pride or ambition, by breaking

[23]

etiquettes is a positive force—and exactly for this reason writing, as self-assertion, is for me something suspect. My game with "them" started in high school, my enemy was our priest who used his secular power in order to enforce upon pupils going to confession every 3 months. My revolt against him resulted from my vice, i.e., my wild egotism. So we are threatened not only from without but also from within and it is obvious for me that I was better protected in my literary career than many colleagues of mine by an innate badness, by my pride or vanité which expected from others exceptional regards due to my talent etc. *The Captive Mind* can be considered as a release of a long repressed fury, as a cold vengeance. I tell you this because I am afraid you ascribe to me too high motives. Writing is suspect since love of truth can go together with an urge to oppose our "I" to the world. If I analyse calmly my scorn of "them" on either side, I cannot see in myself somebody who is for truth or art as opposed to their aims such as power or glory. No. My ambition is higher, I take myself for more intelligent and their power seems to me illusory, their glory miserable. That's all. A spring that jumps when they squeeze it hard. That such writings can be useful to human beings is one of the enigmas of the world. No, I do not want to use rhetorics directed against my person and I recognize that a crazy ego builds up his towers with the material of true pity and compassion. But "we" should not be embellished too much, and not only because of our shunning responsibility but because of our métier which is a pursuit of prestige much higher than that of the politicians. The only remedy is to convey—something important, but always with a danger of self-delusion as to our importance. Forgive me. Matters look differently for you, I am sure, and much of what I am saying you probably had to resolve in the first years of your monastic life.

So back to reality. The Party in Poland made of late a sort of proscription list, placing on it writers who had created in 1957 a review called *Europa*. As to their daring and folly: they unearthed my translation of Robert Browning's "The lost leader"* and wanted to print it in the first issue. That old poem has today over there an explosive meaning and I had to telegraph to Warsaw in order to dissuade them. *Europa*, however, was still-born: censorship forbade it. The Russians are very sensitive, in view of the fact that Polish periodicals of last years often have been hand-copied and translated by youth in Russia, so censorship in Poland is afraid of interventions. Now the Party makes pay to *Europa* group and the first name on the list is that of Alpha, today absolutely uncompromising. (I am very mild compared with him.) The measure aims at taking them by hunger: they are not forbidden to publish but forbidden to hold any jobs in editorial offices or publishing houses which are usual sinecures. The mechanism over there

*Milosz translated "The Lost Leader" in 1945 while living in Cracow.

is such that a writer cannot earn by a "neutral" occupation unless he is not resigned to become one of Orwell's "proles", the income of "average" citizens being very low (quite inverse than in America). This is also impossible for other reasons. Besides, the whole Union of Writers is now under fire and tries to find a modus vivendi with one of the Party scoundrels who blackmails them: either you cooperate with me, or Gamma will come back to power and will take revenge on you. Gamma for the moment is busy with his queer obsession: to prevent, through censorship, mentioning my name in the literary press. So you see all this is parochial and we are among old acquaintances.

The Catholic press is in a relatively better position. The whole problem of Catholicism in Poland: I wish I could discuss it with you one day at length. But without doubt Poland and Hungary are very different from their neighbours and Catholicism counts for very much in that difference. I do not know whether you are familiar with the history of the Greek–Catholic (Uniate) Church. It is strange to think that big planetary issues of today depended once upon success or failure of what Russia considered the greatest threat to its power: the spread of that Church fostered by the Vatican and by the Poles. The last act was staged in 1944/45 when the Soviet authorities converted by force the last areas where that Church was rooted and killed its bishops. Note: converted, officially, into Orthodox religion, with religious hierarchy residing in Moscow.

I have serious difficulties when I start to speak about Russia. Many misunderstandings between me and my friends, French or American. Certainly, I am more interested in Russia than in the Soviet Union. Political struggle masks today the truth about that peculiar civilisation of which the Soviet Union is but one of the avatars. Very few people in the XIXth c. understood or tried to grasp the phenomenon, instruments were lacking and are lacking now, as admirers and foes turn together against anybody who dares to stress the astonishing continuity under changing appearances. I confess, I distrust Russians when they speak about themselves. I distrust, for instance, Berdayev and his escapes into pseudo-mystical fogs. And how much I can admire Boris Pasternak for his human qualities—there is something in his *Doctor Zhivago* which makes me distrustful. I know certain undercurrents. A great Russian poet, Alexander Blok, wrote immediately after the Revolution a famous poem "The dozen" in which revolutionary soldiers march in empty streets and "in white wreath of roses, before them Jesus Christ". Crucified Russia, as the Saviour of mankind, as a chosen nation opening the paths to true Christianity through suffering, makes part of Dostoyevsky's historiosophy and appears in many other authors—also, in a discreet form, in Pasternak.

But a collective body, a human society, cannot be the Saviour. A dream about collective purity achieved thanks to collective suffering is just a dream and in practice it leads to bestiality. I say that as translator of Simone Weil who was as un-Russian as possible. Geoffrey Gorer* pretends that there was only one society based upon the principle of sin—as opposed to Western society based upon the principle of guilt—and that was Czarist Russia. Here he hits the nail, I feel. Guilt is individual, it is my guilt. Sin is universal—not I am guilty but society† and I can be saved not through my effort (Grace given to me) but by the collective of which I am a particle. That's why they are always in search of the Kingdom of God, but placed in time, substituting for it Communism or, perhaps, in the future, another type of eschatology. But personal responsibility is dissolved and I witnessed in 1945 murders committed by Russian soldiers with a deep feeling of sin, but without any feeling of personal guilt whatever. Are you not stricken by passivity of Zhivago, by his being completly submerged in Russia, to the extent that his 3 successive wives are transformed into paysage? By his writing under the spell of inspiration but lack of a moment when a man says to himself: Well, I shall perish, but I shall leave something which will bear fruit in a proper

*Geoffrey Gorer (1905–85) was a cultural anthropologist and controversial social critic.

† Or rather, the Universe. [Milosz's note]

time? Russians to this day detest Marquis Astolphe de Custine* but I am afraid this is because in his voyage in 1839 he guessed many of their secrets. Do not accuse me of being unjust towards Pasternak. His novel is an act, with full conscience of the risk. But a writer expresses trends and attitudes which are stronger than his conscience. During a bombardment in Moscow a Pole asked a crowd looking at the sky why they do not hide themselves in the metro and received the following answer: Nitchevo, we are many. This is splendid as humility: my death does not count. But dangers are tremendous as this means also: my guilt does not count.

There is an archetype of Polish attitude towards Russians, a sort of fascination with Russians as human beings but a categorical rejection of "Russianity", the best example of which is Joseph Conrad's novel *Under Western Eyes.* I am not ashamed to find in myself that archetype as this is not nationalism and does not come, I hope, from wounded patriotic feelings (my patriotism is doubtful). For me Russia is a sad affair, has been a sad affair since its beginnings in the XVth c., different from other countries and continents not by its crimes—history of our planet is criminal—but by a persisting myth of a collective pseudo-Christ. Peoples should not suffer too much. They should be able to produce from time to time a Rabelais or comment on sadness of our

*Marquis Astolphe de Custine (1790–1857), novelist and travel writer best known for *La Russie en 1839.*

fate as Cervantes did. If they suffer too much, obsessed by sin of the Universe, they look for imaginary accomplishment, and, en attendant, one goes to the police to denounce his best friend. After all, Karl Marx, with all his exaggerations, was not perhaps so stupid—I do not know whether you have heard of his being one of the most virulent russophobes of the XIXth c.—of course, those writings of his are censored in Moscow and do not reach the public. I wish all the best to the Russians but am profoundly sceptical.

Dear Merton, I would like to contribute to that oeuvre which you serve too. I have been impregnated with a feeling of that duty since my (very important for me) contact with Oscar Milosz in Paris in 1934, in spite of all my craziness and errings. Yet for a writer this is not simple. A friend of mine reproaches me that I never write what I really think, that I am a dialectician, always speaking through the hat, perhaps a coward. I concede he is right to a certain extent. But one has to be *rusé* as human limitations are great and what our readers would reject when said in an outright way, they swallow hidden in a pill which does not shock their snobbery. This principle I apply in a limited extent only, being besides practically helpless before the Western public from which I am separated not only by the barrier of language. As to my Catholicism, this is perhaps a subject for a whole letter. In any case few people suspect my basically religious interests and I have never been ranged among

"Catholic writers". Which, strategically, is perhaps better. We are obliged to bear witness? But of what? That we pray to have faith? This problem—how much we should say openly—is always present in my thoughts.

I just received your books. Thank you. I notice that "St. Malachy" in the *Tears of the Blind Lions* is what I translated a few years ago. In *Prometheus* you are unjust, it seems to me. If one is for Dante, one cannot be against Prometheus as fire in Heraclitus, probably in the Promethean myth, in Dante, has a symbolic meaning and is the same as the fiery pneuma of the New Testament. Lumière incorporelle of some medieval philosophers. This tradition goes on through centuries. I have sent you *Sur les bords de l'Issa* and have a book of Alpha prepared—I am always slow and late with my tasks and correspondence.

Today is Great Saturday. I send you my fraternal wishes of joy.

Czeslaw Milosz

And yet, I continue. This is a beautiful Easter day. Tits before the house are busy with their nests in boxes I had placed on trees. I mentioned in my letter the Valka camp near Nürnberg. A few years ago, prodded by the editor of *Kultura*, I visited that camp (a wasteland of hopeless waiting, dirt, theft, drunkenness) and wrote an article which was reprinted in Germany and in Canada. In France I did not succeed to place it. The question of refugees is pas bien, offending the prestige, as it is obvious that only les desequilibrés escape from their countries (imagine Sartre writing on refugees!). This in spite of the fact that France is ten times more humane and hospitable to them than Germany. The matter was different with mass migration of Hungarians after 1956, there was a feeling of Western guilt. In any case only Israel has a planned action of resettlement of newcomers; national tie. I should have gone to Valka in 1958. I did not. For egoistic reasons: I do not want to know, to be aware of the fate of some humans and at the same time to be a victim of illusion that an article can help. And no strength to enter that jungle: the fate of that small fry escaping from Czechoslovakia or Poland etc. is in the hands of various secret services, consular offices etc. and people who refuse to be useful are thrown into a camp rotting there for years with this, the heaviest punition: work is forbidden (they have no documents and no permission to work—the right to work is well guarded in our Western world). I have always dissuaded people from Poland from escaping; in individual cases this can bring good results but rarely. To this day I remember the story of two young Rumanians who were starving in Paris so they decided to make a hold-up in an apartment of a rich aristocratic lady, also Rumanian. When besieged by police, one committed suicide, another was killed, defending himself to the last bullet.

As to communist countries, sociological processes going on there are so complex that not only the West does not understand them but they escape the analytical ability of observers who live there. Our instruments are primitive. And a constant danger is a division made often here into "Communists" and "Non-communists". Some friends of mine belong to the Party but their views are not different from my views.

I shall try to translate some of my poems and send them to you. Meanwhile I enclose a copy of my poem translated into French by Oscar Milosz.* I wrote it when I was 23 years old. Later on I went through historical spasms and turmoils.

CM

I forgot. I have met in Paris a few years ago Victoria Ocampo. *Sur* published an essay of mine. The trouble is I am inefficient in writing for the Western public, in fact I am fond of printer's ink but have to be forced or prodded and translations are for me a nightmare.

I decided to take Naomi Burton as my agent and am very grateful for suggestion. I shall write to her soon.

Of your books I have read for the moment *Monastic Peace*, *Prometheus* and several poems. I did not like the beginning of *Monastic Peace*. In my opinion, since the book is for a layman,

*"The Song," 1934.

it should have a more "strategic" opening: many things important can be sometimes lost through the language of devotional literature. This is my impression of a Caliban. But next chapters found of great interest and profited from that reading—the most from pages 41, 42, 43. I see the purpose and it seems to me the best is what stresses harshness of vocation. In your poems I am sensitive to your "choral" rhythm. Perhaps those are my personal inclinations. I have tried to write verse as "naked" as possible, being against (or incapable of) involved imagery. A certain equilibrium between imagery and "discours" should be found—for this reason I am not fond of contemporary French poetry. Your volume has a great advantage: unity of subject—and not only unity of "personality" which is current. For the moment I like the best St. Malachy, being familiar to me as translator, also Song, The Reader, Senescente Mundo. Unity of subject gives or recreates a human situation, your situation face to the world. And mutual movement between your poetry and prose.

I wrote *The Captive Mind* in 1951 but before, in 1947, I had written it in verse*—a very malicious long treatise in iambic verse—the idea of form came probably from Auden's "New Year's Letter". That vicious poem appeared in Poland in 1948 in a literary magazine, as one of the last possibilities before the big Stalinist "frost". I

---

*Treatise on Morals, 1948. No translation has been published in English.

am on the side of poetry which is nourished not by itself.

As you see, I take much pleasure from writing to you and indulging in conversation which shows to you my egotistic preoccupations—how to get rid of them?

※

Dear Milosz:

The only trouble with receiving letters as good and full as yours is that it is a long time before one can answer worthily. I am grateful for your fine letter, which contains so much. In the meantime I have been reading the two books and the *Broken Mirror*. About this more later. I will have much to say.

First, your questions about the "Innocent Bystander".—I hope the fact of my not answering them has not mattered. I leave to you the choice of word for Bystander, and you have probably chosen satisfactorily. In English the special implication is that of one who stands by while a crime is being committed. I am glad you can use it in *Kultura*, but I feel ashamed of it when I realize that it may be read by people who have a real problem. As for myself, I think the problem is still real enough for me to be able to write about it with feeling. I am more and more convinced every day that it is a religious as well as a civil obligation to be discontented with ready-made answers—no matter where they may come from. How much longer can the world subsist on institutional slogans?

Reading the *Broken Mirror* I was moved by the sense of real kinship with most of the writers. Underneath the institutional shells which distinguish us, we have the same ardent desire for truth, for peace, for sanity in life, for reality, for sincerity. But the trouble is that our very efforts to attain these things tend to harden and make more rigid the institutional shell. And a turtle without a shell is not likely to lead a happy life, especially in a world like ours. But perhaps the trouble is that we imagine ourselves turtles. I speak here of the Polish writers in the *Broken Mirror*.* I could not seem to spot any of them as Alpha, though I was looking for him. (You did not send me his book, or at any rate I did not get it.) I thought Brandys's story the "Defense of Granada" was a very good piece and of course I felt very much involved in it, it grips one's sympathies. Parts of Woroszylski's "Notes for a Biography" are also very convincing and sympathetic. I liked perhaps best the notes of Jan Strzelecki. The story by Tadeusz Rozewicz seemed to me to be quite bad—like

* *The Broken Mirror* includes essays by Tadeusz Rozewicz ("The New Philosophical School"); Kazimierz Brandys ("The Defense of Granada"); Zbigniew Herbert ("The Philosopher's Den"); Wiktor Woroszylski ("Notes for a Biography"); Pawel Hertz ("Recollections from the House of the Dead"); Leszek Kolakowski ("Permanent and Transitory Aspects of Marxism"); and Jan Strzelecki ("Notes: 1950–1953").

a contribution to a college humor magazine in this country: one that we would never have published in the *Columbia Jester*. Pawel Hertz was talking about events and groups of which I know nothing and I could not really appreciate his article. I have not yet read the other two pieces. But all in all I feel the greatest sympathy and sense of kinship with most of those writers, apart from the fact that their commitments are so . . . quite alien to me. Be sure to send me Alpha's book. I think often of him, and admire him. I feel deeply for his predicament, and I pray for him. And for all the Polish writers.

Now about your own books. I suppose it is not strange that your younger earthy and cosmic self should be so sharply divided from the later political self. *Sur les bords de l'Issa* is admirably alive, rich in all kinds of archetypal material, with a deep vegetative substratum that gives it a great fertility of meanings. Your lyrical poem falls into the same category. It [strikes] me that this element in your being is very essential to you and that you will not produce your greatest work without it. Its absence from the *Seizure of Power* is one of the things that makes the latter simply a routine job. Of course it is hard to see how ancient pagan naturalistic remnants from archaic Lithuanian peasant culture could be fitted into the tragic story of Warsaw. The fact is that the *Seizure of Power*, though very impressive in patches, did not seem to [hold] together well. You do not seem sure of yourself in it and your statement that you do not like the novel as a literary form by no means surprises me. Yet I think perhaps one day you may go over the same material and write a great novel. I think the *Seizure of Power* suffers from a lack of perspective, and from a natural inability to *assimilate* all the awful elements that had to go into it. One day when you have come to see it all in a unified way, it may turn out quite differently.

I am going to have to go into Simone Weil a little. My acquaintance with her is superficial. As for Providence: certainly I think the glib clichés that are made about the will of God are enough to make anyone lose his faith. Such clichés are still possible in America but I don't see how they can still survive in Europe, at least for anyone who has seen a concentration camp. For my part, I have given up my compulsive need to answer such questions neatly. It is safer and cleaner to remain inarticulate, and does more honor to God. I think the reason why we cannot see Providence at work in our world is that it is much too simple. Our notions of Providence are too complicated and too human: a question of ends and means, and why this means to this end? God wills this *for* this purpose. . . . Whatever the mystery of Providence may be I think it is more direct and more brutal in a way. But that is never evident as long as we think of God apart from the people in the concentration camp, "permitting them to be there for their own good" (time out while I vomit). Actually it is God Himself who is in the concentration camp. That is, of course, it is Christ. Not in the collective sense, but especially in the defilement and destruction of each individual soul, there is the renewal of the Crucifixion. This of course is familiar, I mean the words are familiar. People understand them to mean that a man in a concentration camp who remembers to renew his morning offering suffers like and even, in some juridical sense, with Christ. But the point is whether he renews the morning offering or not, or whether he is a sinner, he *is* Christ. That this is not understood even by religious people: that it cannot be comprehended by the others, and that the last one to be able to understand it, so to speak, is "Christ" Himself . . . Providence is not *for* this hidden Christ. He Himself is His own Providence. In us. Insofar as we are Christ, we are our own Providence. The thing is then not to struggle to work out the "laws" of a mysterious force alien to us and utterly outside us, but to come to terms with what is inmost in our own selves, the very depth of our own being. No matter what our "Providence" may have in store for us, on the surface of life (and this inner Providence is not really so directly concerned with the surface of life) what is within, inaccessible to the evil will of others, is always good unless we ourselves deliberately cut ourselves off from it. As for those who are too shattered to do anything about it one way or the other, they are lifted, in pieces, into heaven and find themselves together there with no sense of how it might have been possible.

When you talk about group action you say what most concerns me, because it is something I know nothing at all about. Even as a Catholic I am a complete lone wolf, and not as independent as I might seem to be, yet not integrated in anything else either. As you say, I represent my own life. But not as I ought to. I have still too much reflected the kind of person others may have assumed I ought to be. I am reaching a happy and dangerous age when I want to smash that image above all. But that is not the kind of thing that is likely to be viewed with favor. Nor do I have any idea of what way the road will take. But as far as solidarity with other people goes, I am committed to nothing except a very simple and elemental kind of solidarity, which is perhaps without significance politically, but which is I feel the only kind which works at all. That is to pick out the people whom I recognize in a crowd and hail them and rejoice with them for a moment that we speak the same language. Whether they be communists or whatever else they may be. Whatever they may believe on the surface, whatever may be the formulas to which they are committed. I am less and less worried by what people say or think they say: and more and more concerned with what they and I are able to be. I am not convinced that anybody is really able to say what he means any more, except insofar as he talks about himself.

And even there it is very difficult. What do any of us "mean" when we talk politics?

And then Russia. I was very interested in what you said about the Russians. I am remote from all that. I have read a few books, I like Dostoevsky, and as you say there is a kind of craziness, a collective myth which strikes one as insincere. An uncharitable judgment: but perhaps there is an awful lot of old man Karamazov in all the Russians—the barefaced liar who will accuse himself of everything and mean nothing. Who just wants to talk. Yet I am very taken with Berdyaev. He is certainly too glib. His explanations and intuitions come up with a suspicious readiness, and he is always inexhaustible. But I find much less of the pseudo-mystic, or rather gnostic, in his later works. As time goes on he seems to me to get more and more solid. *The Meaning of Creation*, one of his earliest books, is one of the most fruitful, the most dangerous and the least reliable at the same time. But a late one like *Solitude and Society** is, I think, almost perfect in its kind. As for Pasternak, of course what you say about Zhivago is true: he floats passively through the backwaters of history. But one does not hold it against him.

There has been an interesting attack on Pasternak by

*Nicholai Berdyaev, *The Meaning of the Creative Act*, translated by D. A. Lowrie. The work first appeared in Russian in 1916. *Solitude and Society*, translated by George Reavey (London: G. Bles, 1938), appeared in Russian in 1934.

Deutscher, a biographer of Stalin, and a crypto-Marxist in this country. I do not mean that he is a "Communist Spy," but that he is one of those solid American intellectuals who have dimly realized the insecurity of this country, culturally, intellectually and politically, and secretly admire Russia for what they imagine to be pragmatic reasons. (It has worked.) There is, in formation, a whole body of potential "new men" in American universities and even in business circles: men without heads and without imagination, with three or four eyes and iron teeth, who are secretly in love with the concept of a vast managerial society. One day we are going to wake up and find America and Russia in bed together (forgive the unmonastic image) and realize that they were happily married all along. It is then that the rest of us are going to have to sort ourselves out and find out if there remains, for us, a little fresh air somewhere in the universe. Neither you nor I are, I think, destined to be managers. I feel much more in common with the Polish writers of the *Broken Mirror* than with an enormously large percentage of business and advertising men in this country: and they in their turn are simply another version of Dr Faul* (is he real?)

About Prometheus—I wonder if you interpreted it correctly? I have nothing against fire. Certainly it is the fire of the spirit: my objection is that it does not have to be stolen,

*Doktor Faul is the pseudonym of a man described in Kazimierz Brandys's "The Defense of Granada," in *The Broken Mirror*.

and that it cannot be successfully stolen. It has been already given, and Promotheus's climb, defeat and despair is all in his own imagination. That is the tragedy. He had the fire already.

Finally, I think it is eminently good that you, especially as a Pole, are not listed as a Catholic writer pure and simple. You can do much more good that way. Categories are of very little use, and often to be clearly labelled is equivalent to being silenced.

I want to get this letter out today, so I will write no more for the moment. How are you getting along with Naomi Burton? She seems to think you are all tied up with Knopf. I did not understand her. I still hope you will get a good translator. The fact that you write for Poland is not too important. What you write for Poland will be read with interest everywhere. You do not have to change your mental image of your audience. The audience will take care of itself.

All you wrote about Valka seemed to me supremely important. These are things we have to think about and write about and do something about; otherwise we are not writers but innocent (?) bystanders. Especially shameful is this business of "using" these people for a cause, and if they cannot be used, then leaving them to rot. How clear it is that on both sides they are very much the same, and that the dividing lines are not where they appear to be.

God bless you and your family. You are wise even in your

insecurity, for today insecurity and wisdom are inseparable.
I keep you in my Mass and in my prayers. Pray for me too,
please. And remember me to Alpha, and send me his book
if you can.

Faithfully in Christ

* * *

July 16, 1959

Dear Merton,

After I got your last letter I felt an urge to answer immediately but it is better I did not. One should avoid ba-
vardage and your time should be spared. You are for me
important, I feel in you a friend with whom I can be
completely frank. The trouble is I have never been used to
frankness. I go very rarely to confession, once every few
years, I do not know how to do that and it seems to me
afterwards that I was lying. It does not mean I am tepid
but of little faith and loathing my nature (which is a pre-
text not to see particular sins). So many problems. But I
hope, I feel, I met in you somebody who will help me one
day—this is a hope of a deeper contact and of complete
openness on my part. Probably not now, I just write a few
words. The last poem I wrote is entitled "Conversations
for Easter 1620"—a dialogue between an old gentleman
and the spirit of doubt, but with rhymes and in the old

Polish, so untranslatable. We have no "metaphysical poets", so one can re-create them ex post—though not for
the sake of a literary game.

Prometheus. This is exactly the subject of work which
plays in Poland the same role as "Faust" in Germany—*The
Forefathers* by Mickiewicz.* Action in a tsarist prison on
Christmas Eve. A young prisoner is a Prometheus—he cannot bear sufferings of mankind and starts a battle with
God—in splendid verse. The scene of his "transe" has as its
accompaniment voices of good spirits and bad spirits who
fight for his soul. When he reaches the peak of satanic pride
(because he loves miserable humanity) he is saved by prayer
of an obscure humble priest. Perhaps this work of the beginning of the XIXth c., known practically by heart, had
something to do with my not grasping the sense of your
text. Yet I am not sure as to Prometheus himself. I have felt
attraction of the Manichaean tradition. For S. Weil Prometheus was a prefiguration of Christ.

No, I do not write in this letter what I would like to
write. Pray for Alpha. From what I have heard of late he is
in a very bad fix. Incessantly drunk, in chaos, despair, his
homosexuality etc. I have not read in French his book I had
sent you. I suppose this is not especially good. He is in a

*Adam Mickiewicz (1798–1855), Lithuanian-born, considered the great poet of
Polish romanticism. *Forefather's Eve* (1823) is a long, dramatic poem, *Pan Tadeusz*,
an epic tale of life among Polish and Lithuanian gentry, is his most famous work.

critical period, either he gets out of it or. I repeat what I have heard from very honest people. He needs your help.

As to myself, I doubt whether writing and publishing can go together with purity of heart. Writing is after all a constant masquerade and a constant revenge of our ego, even if we have better intentions. Our image in the eyes of others. Sometimes it seems to me that I am no more arrogant and easily taken in by flattery, then I think I simply instilled myself in my feeling of superiority, so even unfavorable opinions do not hurt me so much as before. This is a very bad profession and I have seen pride, or vanity, even in the wisest of my confreres. How should one manage this? On 14 juillet I got drunk and with all the vices possible a violent aggressivity, impertinence, showed up—looking for street bagarre etc. I am a complete fool who pretends to be somebody else.

Family life creates problems, especially children—I suffer noticing in them what is worst in me and should not have been perpetuated, things which condemned me to be a writer i.e. invalid in a sense. Is not so that I suffer because my self-love suffers, in the children I see myself unmasqued. How do you solve this in the monastery, what is the point of view of the Catholic doctrine—I mean organic predestination—there are people of good grain and of bad grain and I am sceptical as to pedagogy, efforts of will—there is a limit. I do not mean an innate propensity to evil. No. I mean physical inability of total opening towards the others, of altruism, of charity for instance, which does not exclude short moments of good intentions.

I am finishing a book, with great pain.* Cannot write that last chapter. In *Sign of Jonas* I found what you say on the 22nd Sunday after Pentecost—words of St. Hilary on Caesar (from the Night Office). This can help me. The subject of that last chapter is my 5 years in the service of the Polish communist government or rather a portrait of a friend who had a decisive influence upon me in that time.† Of course I do not want to write gossip but to present a certain philosophical, so to say, situation. This is so difficult because I cannot grasp all the contradictory motives and all the reasons—why I was so fascinated by his mind. My friend (he died a year ago from a heart attack) was a master of Ketman which I tried to describe in the *Captive Mind*. He was a professor of Marxist philosophy at the Warsaw University and in a special Party school. Pretending, lying all the time, he was not, in fact, a Marxist but a Hegelian, besides of a very peculiar brand. A sort of permanent comedian, rather vile but very loyal towards friends. Despised

*It later appeared in English as *Native Realm: A Search for Self-definition*, 1968.

†The chapter entitled "Tiger" is a portrait of Juliusz Tadeusz Kronski, a professor and a Hegelian, whom Milosz depicts as a philosopher of Ketman. In *The Captive Mind*, Milosz borrows the term "Ketman" from the Muslim religious practice of mental reservation in unfriendly regimes and applies it to the way Eastern Europeans masquerade to hide their true beliefs and values as a way of surviving in a "Party"-dominated system.

materialist philosophy (as you know in so-called dialectical materialism "dialectics" and "materialism" do not go very well together, there is an internal contradiction). Used to say also that only idiots do not believe in immortality of soul. Tortured by his ambition, humiliated, scared. Died reading *Esthetics* of Hegel and Proust.

To have nothing which belongs to Caesar, as St. Hilary advises? Yes, but there is a question of action. I lived through morally difficult years—years you describe in *Sign of Jonas*—in Washington D.C. (especially 1949). And now, when I look back, I see a mixture of bad and of good in my clinging to Poland. (It was very easy to break and remain in the States.) Had I met you then—perhaps things would have been different but I doubt, I was in a vicious circle. Literature belongs to the world and the world is Caesar's. I was not mature enough to live by contemplation—struggle, or an illusion of struggle, is more invigorating. I was in a black despair and looked for advice of Albert Einstein, whom I knew. He felt my breaking would be harmful for my writing (he was against exile by principle) and not honest. My decision of leaving the States was influenced by him but even more so by my friend-Hegelian (inevitability of Russian victory, Caesar's rule over the whole world and the only action left to us: cheating Caesar). Later on, in Europe, I could not stand all that reasoning, I loathed my guts. Besides, my story is incredible. Nobody could understand how I escaped from

Poland, in full Stalinism, if they had me already in a trap and were decided to keep me. The secret is that I was helped by a very influential person who hated Stalin, as Stalin had destroyed that person's family. My story was, at a certain point, connected with stories of persons as if taken from *Doctor Zhivago* of Pasternak. Forgive me. There is no need to tell all this. I tell it just to show that I am in trouble when I try to make a sort of distillation, without being too personal, without being even concerned too much with so-called problems of communism—what is important for me is the game with Caesar as the last chapter of my half-biographical book.

I feel deep, deep gratitude for everything which has been given me. And I would like to show my gratitude. I live in expectation—that one day I shall be able to write in such a way that it will be visible. But probably I have to wait. Meanwhile the chapter has to be written. The book in question is for me already a burden. In it there are only hints of gratitude. I have been always perhaps too strategical.

About *Sign of Jonas* in the next letter. I am reading it slowly. From my letter you see perhaps already what is wrong with me and what I need.

Cordially
Czeslaw Milosz

PS I agree with what you say about my writings. I agree, too, with what you say of Providence in our lives. But I cannot get rid of hostility towards the idea of Providence in History. Nature and History, both, seem to me subjected to the terrible necessity, iron necessity, which is the domain of Prince de ce monde. I am revolted against tribal Divinity of the Old Testament. Dislike Bossuet.* Modern interpretations of Divine Pedagogy (Teilhard de Chardin)† repulse me, as crazily optimistic, tinged with Hegel and tutti quanti. It is not so that I would like to understand what is mystery. But one thing is to trace limits of mystery and state clearly where the unsolvable contradiction of existence starts, another thing is to swim in the vague, as, I suspect, the theologians mostly do.

One correction. I do not identify Nature and History and do not ascribe to them the same kind of necessity. "Historical Necessity" of totalitarians is a projection of the XIXth c. scientific outlook in biology etc into the World of Man, which belongs to Nature and does not belong at the same time—that projection is a source of great evil. I have written and published two years ago a long treatise in verse on that subject‡—very few people grasped what it was about

---

*Jacques Bossuet (1627–1704), Jesuit priest and author of sermons and meditations.

†Pierre Teilhard de Chardin (1881–1955), Jesuit priest and anthropologist, author of *The Phenomenon of Man* (1955) and numerous other controversial works on the reconciliation of Christianity and evolution.

‡"Treatise on Poetry," 1957. Short selections from two sections of this poem, "Beautiful Times" and "The Spirit of History," have been translated into English and appear in *The Collected Poems*, 1988.

but my friend-Hegelian, who received the booklet in Warsaw, did. And if History is basically different from Nature, Providence can act through human souls. But without interfering with specific necessity to which History is subjected, without stepping into the realm reserved for the Prince du Mensonge, without helping armies to win battles. Everything here is for me absolutely obscure but I am against Teilhard de Chardin so to say by instinct. And perhaps Prometheus was not an ancestor of modern revolutionaries, perhaps he was in revolt against a heavy, false God, but not against God the Father?

I cannot stop thinking on that. You are right that I am not for history, politics etc. But sometimes contemplation is purified through obstacles, through barriers of the world.

※

Sept. 12, 1959

My Dear Milosz:

First of all thanks for Alpha's book, *Le Samedi Saint.** I read it with interest, and found it competent, but nothing too remarkable. I have passed it on to my publisher urging

*Jerzy Andrzejewski, *La Semaine Sante*, translated by E. Goriely, 1958.

him to put it out in English, which certainly ought to be done. I note what you say about Alpha's predicament, and think of him often—remember him daily at Mass. If he were not nearly in despair there would be something the matter with him: his plight is a sign that he is at least healthy enough to react. The only thing that is to be regretted without qualification is for a man to adapt perfectly to totalitarian society. Then he is indeed beyond hope. Hence we should all be sick in some way. We should all feel near to despair in some sense because this semi-despair is the normal form taken by hope in a time like ours. Hope without any sensible or tangible evidence on which to rest. Hope in spite of the sickness that fills us. Hope married to a firm refusal to accept any palliatives or anything that cheats hope by pretending to relieve apparent despair. And I would add that for you especially hope must mean acceptance of limitations and imperfections and the deceitfulness of a nature that has been wounded and cheated of love and of security: this too we all feel and suffer. Thus we cannot enjoy the luxury of a hope based on our own integrity, our own honesty, our own purity of heart.

Yet on the other hand, our honesty consists in resisting the temptation to submerge our guilt in the collective deluge, and in refusing to be proud that our "hands are dirty" and making that fact a badge of adaptation and success in the totalitarian world. In the end, it comes to the old story that we are sinners, but that this is our hope because sinners are the ones who attract to themselves the infinite compassion of God. To be a sinner, to want to be pure, to remain in patient expectation of the divine mercy and above all to forgive and love others, as best we can, this is what makes us Christians. The great tragedy is that we feel so keenly that love has been twisted out of shape in us and beaten down and crippled. But Christ loves in us, and the compassion of Our Lady keeps her prayer burning like a lamp in the depths of our being. That lamp does not waver. It is the light of the Holy Spirit, invisible, and kept alight by her love for us.

Your piece in *Preuves* is very good reading, and promises that the book will be one of your very best.* I am most eager to have it and to read it. The pages I have seen in the magazine are interesting and moving, and I was deeply impressed by the prophetic insights of Oscar Milosz, who seems to have been most remarkable. I too believe both in the coming destruction and in the coming resurrection of the Church and an age of worldwide Christianity. And I believe these things will happen very fast, and strangely, and

*"Le jeune homme et les secrets," in *Preuves*, 1959: 100, pp. 75–83.

without any apparent struggle on the part of men—I mean without any apparent struggle to bring about the good. Rather it will all take place against the concerted efforts of the whole human race to bring about evil and despair. The glory will belong not to man but to God.

I still do not share your scruples about writing, though lately I have been thinking of giving it up for a while, and seeking a more austere and solitary kind of existence (I go through that cycle frequently, as you have seen in the *S. of Jonas*, but this time it is more serious. I will probably never give up writing definitively. I have just been finishing another book, *The Inner Experience**—a wider deeper view of the same thing, contemplation, with more reference to oriental ideas. There is to me nothing but this that counts, but everything can enter into it. You are right to feel a certain shame about writing. I do too, but always too late—five years after a book has appeared I wish I had never been such a fool as to write it. But when I am writing it I think it is good. If we were not all fools we would never accomplish anything at all. As to people of good grain and bad grain, I do not have easy answers, but again I think a great deal depends on love, and when people are loved they change. But

---

*This book was never published. Selections have appeared in William H. Shannon's *Thomas Merton's Dark Path: The Inner Experience of a Contemplative* (1981) and in Lawrence Cunningham's *Thomas Merton: Spiritual Master*. Individual chapters were published in *Cisterian Studies* 18–19 (1983–84).

what is happening in the world today is a wholesale collapse of man's capacity to love. He has been submerged under material concerns, and by the fantastic proliferation of men and things all around him, so that there are so many of everything that one lives in a state of constant bewilderment and fear. One cannot begin to commit himself to any definite love, because the whole game is too complex and too hazardous and one has lost all focus. So we are carried away by the whirlwind, and our children are even more helpless than we ourselves. It is the basic *helplessness* of man coming out at the moment of his greatest power over things other than himself that has precipitated this moral crisis. But there have always been this fear of helplessness, this impatience and panic which makes a man want to assure himself of his power before he relaxes and allows himself to love. And so he gets carried away with his projects to remind himself that he exists, and can never allow himself to love fully—to get away from himself. Who is to blame? Everyone. The answer—the only answer I know—is that of Staretz Zossima in *The Brothers Karamazov*—to be responsible to everybody, to take upon oneself *all* the guilt—but I don't know what that means. It is romantic, and I believe it is true. But what is it? Behind it all is the secret that love has an infinite power, and its power, once released, can in an instant destroy and swallow up all hatred, all evil, all injustice, all that is diabolical. That is the meaning of calvary. I don't expect to wake up one morning and find that I am doing this all by myself. Yet if we understood the Mass, that is what it is about. Unfortunately, there is the veil of incomprehensibility suspended before the mystery by the presence and actions of the *bien-pensants* who need no mercy because they have no guilt (?). That is what we all secretly aspire to be, unfortunately, and thank God He does not allow it.

I hope you have got that last chapter satisfactorily down on paper, and if you have had to wrestle with it, it will certainly be good. The days in Red Poland would obviously be the hardest to write about, and the most important. You probably have not completely succeeded, and yet it will be excellent. By the way, Stephen Spender's wife stopped by here, and I mentioned your name. She immediately exclaimed "Oh, the *Captive Mind.*" She is tremendously impressed with it, as is everybody. As for your friend who practised Ketman, that is certainly one form of honesty, and perhaps an admirable one. It is certainly a form of justice, and a providential kind of justice. If there is one ambition we should allow ourselves, and one form of strength, it is perhaps this kind of wholehearted irony, to *be* a complete piece of systematic irony in the middle of the totalitarian lie—or the capitalist one. And even the official religious one. But that is delicate, and thank God not yet necessary. It might be in Spain.

It gets back to the fact that we all have our game with Caesar, the Little Father who is no longer human and who therefore *ought* to be cheated, in the name of humanity. I have been reading William Blake again. His reply to Caesar seems like psychosis, but it is valid and consistent and prophetic: and involves no Ketman except perhaps a very little of it, on the surface, with some of his "friends" who had money but did not understand him. And this did not get into any of his writing. And I am reading Job with the novices. Maybe the Old Testament is God Himself playing Ketman. For me, seen in the light of Job, the Old Testament presents no special problem. As for Bossuet I have always had an instinctive revulsion for everything he represents. Teilhard de Chardin I have not read.

It is a shame that you write poems that cannot be translated, but it is most important that you continue to do so. Important for you, and for poetry, and for Poland. And I think Einstein's advice was fortunate at the time, if you had simply stayed here everything might have gone to pot.

I am sending you a couple of offprints, under separate cover. I cannot remember if I sent you the Pasternak article already. Write whenever and however you please, it is very good to have your letters and to talk with you, any time, always. I keep you in my prayers. Forgive this very rambling letter, much of which may perhaps turn out to be silly. Meanwhile I am eager to hear what you think about *Jonas*, though that is now ten years ago and I have changed a lot in many ways. Am less innocent, and what was said there quietly and gently is now coming out in a more crucial and definitive form, so that now I need many prayers. In my own way, I have the same problem that everyone has everywhere. God bless you.

Faithfully in Christ
Tom Merton

※

Dear Merton,

Your letters give me always joy. I should tell you something of my impressions from my reading *Sign of Jonas*. I believe that as every reader of your books I am so to say double. Don't blame me for being very practical or empirical. So, judging from an empirical point of view, I feel your book is useful as it shows that a kind of life considered in general as monotonous or gray can be rich and full of experiences. For the contemporary public every discovery of such a new world, far from Pascalian "divertissements" is healthy. It is probable that I am more and more utilitarian in my approach to literature, but in a special sense, a new code of exigencies in our period of "ricanement" in art and literature is difficult to formulate. François Mauriac* (whose novels I dislike) expressed well his reaction to the face of Vladimir Nabokov on the television screen: "Quelle leçon! Quelle expérience, et dont j'ai rêvé durant la nuit: deux visages se sont succédé: celui de Vladimir Nabokow, l'auteur de *Lolita*, tel que nous pouvions l'imaginer, d'une respectabilité, d'une correction a faire frémir, faite a souhait pour mettre en confiance les petites filles. Et puis un autre visage a paru, le plus spirituel que j'ai jamais admiré sur l'écran, j'entends 'spirituel' au sens propre. C'est un esprit qui se manifeste ici, celui de Raymond Aron."†

So, *The Sign of Jonas* is useful and left me first of all many images—hills, forests, dormitories—as a sufficient scene of life. I have been thinking of you when reading *The Cloud of Unknowing*‡ or rather its translation into modern English made by Quakers of Pendle Hill (I was there once in 1947)—I was thinking of life of many anonymous monks in the XIVth c. at the same time.

*François Mauriac (1885–1970), novelist, philosopher, and theologian.

†Raymond Aron (1905–83), sociologist and philosopher of history. He was a friend and then an antagonist of Sartre's. Aron edited *Preuves*, which published Milosz's essay on Camus in 1960.

‡*The Cloud of Unknowing*, written by an English monk in the late fourteenth century, stresses love over understanding or the attempt to break through the cloud of unknowing that separates God and humanity.

But usefulness of your book is limited for somebody who is seriously interested in "anatomy of faith" if you permit that expression, somewhat improper. I guess that many readers of yours belong to that category. That question tortures today many people: how one believes, what are the contents of faith, in any case those translatable into notions and images. The problem is very difficult: literature is too subjective, theological treatises too abstract. Your diary describes your internal country in its results, for whoever comes from outside that country exists, which is much, but remains mysterious—of course it is mysterious for you too, but I use the word here in a very terre à terre sense. What you describe is like a jungle for people who have never seen one. Probably Bernanos* (whom I read years ago) makes the same impression. This is a problem of difference between noting, as one usually does in a diary, and distilling. The danger in the first case is to be "trop touffu", in the second to be aphoristic or dry, and if I speak about that here it is because I am looking for solutions.

My other side—simply of a reader—cannot be separated from those "apologetic" considerations. For a while I inhabited that part of Kentucky and I was in your presence, but, to resume shortly my feeling, I was waiting for something—nothing sensational and dramatic—to happen,

*George Bernanos (1888–1948), author of *Journal d'un curé de campagne* (1936) (*Diary of a Country Priest*) and *Dialogue des Carmélites*.

namely a kind of summa from time to time, and not only in terms of stages of your develoment. To be more clear, for instance nature in your book is contaminating, one is under its spell, but it is a background, nature is spiritualized and I waited for a moment when you meet her not only in its beauty or calm but also in its immutability of law: a dead beetle on your path. In other words, less macrocosm, more microcosm. This is but one instance. The fact is that Catholic literature rarely comes across the barrier to reach domains of "lay" literature, I understand your effort and your vocation to go across but *The Sign of Jonas*, as it is a diary, remains in the fortress. It seems to me that the barrier is largely illusory, that novels such as those of Graham Greene or François Mauriac belong to the past (in them religion is added, as a Deus ex machina), that new means can be tried. I suppose I was waiting until the last page of your book for something which by definition had been excluded in advance, so I am very unjust but I have to tell you frankly that I did not read your book as one reads a story and in this I am in agreement with your real purpose. To put it in a naïve way: I waited for some answers to many theological questions but answers not abstract as in a theological treatise, just on that border between the intellect and our imagination, a border so rarely explored today in religious thinking: we lack an image of the world, ordered by religion, while Middle Ages had such an image. This was not the aim of your diary and I have no reason to demand from one book of yours what can be demanded from all your work. But a reader (I can judge by introspection only) is eager to learn (gradually) what is the image of the world in Thomas Merton. In a period when the image accepted by majority is clear: empty Sky, no pity, stone wasteland, life ended by death. I imagine a reader who says: he possessed a secret, he succeeded in solving the puzzle, his world is harmonious, yet in his diary he tells already about sequences while we would be ready to follow him in 5 volumes through a very vision of the world redeemed by Christ. In how many books we can find it if we exclude books of devotion?

I beg you, do not interpret this as an attempt to convince you to become a theologian in the Dominican tradition. You said very justly that I am the best when I touch the earth, nature, when I am vegetal. I can repay you: you created a new dimension thanks to images, you changed a monastery into something else than it was in literature up to the last times. How to combine two contradictory exigencies I do not know.

I am reading Swedenborg. Not that I intend to become a theosopher. He is amazing and thanks to him I grasped certain things, especially thanks to his theory of correspondences: one sees to what extent the XIXth c. symbolism was based upon it, but used it in a diluted and degenerated form.

Swedenborg can be used as a commentary to Dante. Besides, his example confirms what Simone Weil says about truth absolutely identical in all the mystical writings. It was a great lacune in my education, I should have read Swedenborg years ago.

I am glad that you exist
with love

＊

28.II.60

Dear Merton,

Centuries. Once I wrote a long letter to you but did not send it. First, about your books. You forgive me if I approach them now from a practical angle instead of writing essays of criticism. Since I believe I cannot reach higher than "active contemplation" as you call it in your reappraisal; the practical aspect is for me important. I wish your books had influence and not only upon Roman Catholics. If I cling to such people as you, in spite of my weak faith, it is because I am revolted against that complete craziness one observes today in art and literature and which reflects a more general madness. Of late I saw *Les Nègres* of Jean Genet, already typical by its diabolical skill put to the use of "ricanement". That play opens and ends by a celestial Mozart music just to make the audience better taste two hours of blasphemies and hatred in the middle. Perhaps we approach a time when only groups of monks in monasteries will remain sane. Your books should have influence. Yet I see an obstacle. To put it briefly (too briefly) it is your kind of sensitivity, reinforced probably by your training. Let us take the example of your diary. Every time you speak of Nature, it appears to you as soothing, rich in symbols, as a veil or a curtain. You do not pay much attention to torture and suffering in Nature. You are completely right when you praise Boris Pasternak for his feeling of wholeness, of participation in the mystery of being. But he is so near to you just because of what is for you a danger as it can reduce your influence upon non-Catholics. We live through a time when Manichaeism is particularly strong and one could enumerate many reasons for it—though we do not grasp as yet all the causes. I do not know to what extent a sort of despair at the sight of ruthless necessity in Nature is justified. Yet it exists while it was not known until quite modern times. The distance between man and the rest of Creation was so great that for Descartes too the animal was a machine. Some old Manichaean elements started to revive perhaps in the Reformation but they were mitigated. You can say that overstressed compassion for millions and billions of creatures crushed every second makes part of the modern schism which destroyed quite real barriers between man and animal. But the bitter taste of necessity colours the style of our contemporaries and if Simone Weil is such a force and if she counterbalances many modern follies, it is because she was *une Cathare.* Albert Camus called her (in a letter) "the only great spirit of our time" and Camus undoubtedly was a Manichaean. By the way, I would like to convince you to comment upon *La Chute* de Camus, a very ambiguous book, which is a cry of despair and a treatise on Grace (absent). Perhaps it would be useful if you write a theological commentary. I am far from wishing to convert you to Manichaeism. Only it is so that the palate of your readers is used to very strong sauces and le Prince de ce monde is a constant subject of their reflections. That ruler of Nature and of History (if laws are different, necessity is similar) does not annoy you enough—in your writings. With Pasternak the problem looks a little different, the pressure of historical ruthlessness upon him is so great that symbolism of Nature can be a consolation. Your poetry is based on a music of death and renewal and your sympathy for Pasternak stems from a deep affinity. Your booklet on Christianity of Pasternak is convincing though I am not quite sure whether ce "christianisme diffus" or pan-love-ism is exactly Christian. Perhaps I am wrong and too much under the suggestion of other Russian works, like *The Twelve* of Alexander Blok, with their theodicy and a mixture of historical (revolutionary) and religious tendencies (read an essay of a young Soviet author* "On socialist realism" in the Winter 1960 issue of the quarterly *Dissent*). Nevertheless I risk the opinion that as a writer you should not only understand and deplore the modern gnashing of teeth but to have some complicity with it. People who make so to say a good use of it are so rare, that's why the whole field is invaded by les ricaneurs of Jean Genet type and the fascination with Evil is transformed into a revolt against Redemption. You have to deal with a tough public. What I mean can be illustrated by the poems I am enclosing. Their author, Zbigniew Herbert,† a young Polish poet, a friend of mine, is now on a fellowship in Paris (he lives usually in Warsaw). The translation is mine‡. You shall notice what cruel experience underlays here the poetic image.

I do not remember whether I told you that your "Letter to an innocent bystander" published by *Kultura* had quite an echo. Also letters from the U.S.A., from Americans of Polish origin who otherwise would not perhaps read it. A letter from a Pole of Chicago, whose family for generations was Lutheran. He quotes two authors who led him back to Catholicism: Simone Weil and you. But I think you would

---

*A. Tertz [A. D. Sinyavsky].

†Zbigniew Herbert (1924–) became prominent in the 1950s. Milosz edited *Selected Poems of Zbigniew Herbert* (1968). Other major Herbert collections include *Report from the Besieged City* and *Mr. Cogito* as well as a book of essays, *Still Life with a Bridle*.

‡I am absolutely unable to translate my own poems. [Milosz's note]

be more effective if you did not avoid a certain Manichaean touch. Without doubt you smile at my very low (I recognize it) level of religious consciousness. I have read *The Cloud of Unknowing* with trembling and decided to avoid dangerous aspirations which are beyond my reach. But I speak as somebody from the world and I wish you well.

Alpha is now in Paris. We spent Christmas together in Montgeron. Our relations are very cordial. He says I had the right to write what I wrote of him. The most terrifying is perhaps not the change to which we are subjected but the lack of change, a basic identity of our nature through the time, predestination (biology, genetics is my real terror). Perhaps he was only playing—playing with Catholicism, playing with Communism. The result is that now, after he had left the Communist Party, there is a vacuum and a belief in personal relationships, in personal loyalties only. I try to convey to him my feeling that one should not pour out the baby together with the bath and because of the disillusionment with Communism look for a refuge in an ivory tower, disguised with various paraphernalia. But this is a more or less general mood of Polish writers now. A film made from Alpha's novel *The ashes and the diamond* ran here in Paris. Very good picture, much more honest and superior to the novel. The press was enthusiastic, but no commercial success—the film touches upon questions too difficult for Western average public.

After much sweating I finished my book and it appeared in Polish here in Paris. In New York it is now in the hands of Curtis Brown. The last year I had a proposal from one of the big American universities to come there as a visiting professor. For many reasons I had to decline the offer for the moment, perhaps they would renew it, perhaps not. But I have plenty of work and a project of a new book is slowly growing. I believe it would be mostly concerned with things present in this letter.

Thank you for your last letter. Your letters are very dear to me. I received your books, also the last one, your poems.

In Paris I visit often Mme Bernard Weil, the mother of Simone. She is very old, over eighty, but astonishingly alert and clear-thinking. The death of Albert Camus was a serious blow for her because of a personal friendship and because works of Simone (there are still many manuscripts) appeared in the collection "Espoir" at Gallimard directed by Camus.

Did you read perchance a book on Protestantism by Louis Bouyer*? He is an ex-Protestant minister, now of Oratoire, teaches here at the Institut Catholique and at Notre Dame University in the States. I have met him and was not enchanted, but his book is clear, concise, written in excellent French (I find the French literary style of today awful). I suspect only French theologians write well. Otherwise a

*Louis Bouyer, *Du Protestanisme à l'Eglise*, 1964.

Hellenistic culture of a decadent Alexandria. Bouyer's book is useful, in view of its ecumenic preoccupations.

I do not know how one should finish letters to you, there is this respect for the priest's robe, let me say with brotherly love

Czeslaw Milosz

※

May 6, 1960

Dear Milosz:

It is a shame to make so fine a letter as your last one wait so long for an answer, and yet it is precisely the good letters that take time to answer. Yours required much thought, and I still haven't come through with anything intelligent or worthy of your wise observations.

Not that there is not plenty of resentment in me: but it is not resentment against nature, only against people, institutions and myself. I suppose this is a real defect, or rather a limitation: but actually what it amounts to is that I am in complete and deep complicity with nature, or imagine I am: that nature and I are very good friends, and console one another for the stupidity and the infamy of the human race and its civilization. We at least get along, I say to the trees, and though I am perfectly aware that the spider eats the fly, that the singing of the birds may perhaps have something to do with hatred or pain of which I know nothing, still I can't make much of it. Spiders have always eaten flies and I can shut it out of my consciousness without guilt. It is the spider, not I, that kills and eats the fly. As for snakes, I do not like them much, but I can be neutral and respectful towards them, and find them very beautiful in fact, though this is a recent development. They used to strike me with terror. But they are not evil. I don't find it in myself to generate any horror for nature or a feeling of evil in it. Or myself. There, of course, there is more guilt, and shame. I do not find it at all hard to hate myself, and I am certainly not always charitable about other people, I like to flay them in words, and probably I should feel more guilty about it than I do, because here I sin, and keep on sinning.

At the same time I enjoy and respect Camus, and think I understand him. What you said about *La Chute* struck me very forcibly when I read it: it is a fine piece of Manichaean theology and very applicable to this (Trappist) kind of life. In fact I was able to use it to good effect, perhaps cruelly, in the spiritual direction of a narcissistic novice. But the thing of Camus that really "sends" me is the marvelous short story about the missionary who ends up as a prisoner in the city of salt. There, in a few words, you have a superb ricanement, in theology! And a very salutary piece for Trappists to read, because for generations we have been doing just that kind of thing. I was deeply saddened by his death. In politics I think I am very much inclined to his way of looking at things, and there is in him an honesty and a compassion which belies the toughness of his writing.

Perhaps I am capable of being more sardonic: but my life has been peculiar, and there has been enough effective evasion in it for my sardonic side to be vitiated. I have escaped so much trouble that my ricanement at its best is a bit adolescent. A kind of healthy shame prevents me from really using it, except in the rather silly and innocuous situations in which I slightly shock my fellow priests and religious in matters of no consequence—like sarcasm about liturgical vestments, saint sulpice, pious clichés and other such trivialities.

I am going to have to read Simone Weil. I know she is great and what I have read about her attracts me. Her thought as I have picked it up here and there from the remarks of others is congenial to me. But the books of hers that I have looked at so far have not appealed to me, perhaps because they were in English.

Of course, the funny thing is that I am very frequently accused, here in America and also in England, of being too Manichaean. Perhaps that is why I have obediently tried to mute the rancor that is quite often an undertone in my writing, but perhaps too it is so much of an undertone that I am the only one left who can hear it. And in the end, everyone envies me for being so happy. I do not have the impression of being especially happy, and I am in definite reaction against my surroundings: for a "happy monk" I must admit that I certainly protest a great deal against the monastic Order, and the Order itself thinks I protest a great deal too much. But of course, it must be understood that in an institution like ours even the slightest hint of protest is already too much.

I am willing to admit that in the sight of God I do not protest enough, and that the protests I generally make are always beside the target. I have the impression that when I am indignant in print, I am always indignant about something vague and abstract, and not about something more concrete which I really hate and which I cannot recognize. It is absurd to rave vaguely about "the world", the "modern age", the "times". I suppose I will gradually get over that.

What I get back to, and here you can tell me if my examination of conscience is correct, is that in actual fact my real guilt is for being a bourgeois. I am after all the prisoner of my class, and I tell myself that I don't care if I am. One has to be prisoner of some class or other, and I might as well be what I am instead of going through the ridiculous and pharisaical pretense of being the avant garde of a classless world. But the fact remains that I hate being a bourgeois, and hate the fact that my reaction against it is not a success: simply the bohemian reaction, I suppose, with a new twist, a religious modality.

When all this is said, I find it difficult to be sincerely bitter in the way that you describe, but also the real ricanement people bore me to death. I do not have much interest in Sartre, he puts me to sleep, as if he were deliberately dull: *assommant* is a much better word. He shaves me, as the French say. He beats me over the head with his dullness, though *Huis Clos* strikes me as a good and somewhat puritanical play. The other thing of his I have tried to read, *Nausée*, is drab and stupid.

All that you have said remains unchallenged by these evasive explanations. It is quite true that I ought to speak more with the accents of my time. They are serious, they are not just a pose, the bitterness of people is not just something to be dismissed. I detest the fake optimism that is current in America, including in American religion. I shall continue to think about these things. The books of mine you have read belong however to a sort of Edenic period in my life, and what is later is more sardonic. I think the last poems will prove that statement, including the "Elegy for the Five Old Ladies."

I like the poems of Zbigniew Herbert, especially "At the Gates of the Valley." It is fine, and not just negative: there is a kind of pity in its contempt, its refusal of compassion. Do you know a few of Dylan Thomas' poems about death, including the Refusal to Mourn for a Girl Burned in an Air Raid*—that too is tremendous. I have recently been reading the poems of Brecht, and until one gets to the absurd and conventional moral, the "happy ending", they too are tough and convincing. I like the one especially where the Vögelein schwiegen im walde . . . Why not let Zbigniew Herbert's poems be submitted to New Directions for their yearly anthology—I will copy them out and touch up the word order a bit, it might go. Let me know if you approve.

Whether or not you should come to America depends on a lot of things, but the atmosphere of this country is singularly unstimulating. Why live among lotus eaters and conformists, and such conformists. Never was there a place where freedom was so much an illusion. But if you do come, then I would have the pleasure of talking to you down here, I hope. For that reason I hope you will come. But for the rest you will find here no imagination, nothing but people counting, counting and counting, whether with giant machines, or on their stupid fingers. All they know how to do is count. I wish you could see one good book, though, that is unknown, by my friend Robert Lax— *The Circus in the Sun*. I'll ask him to send you a review copy for *Kultura*. It

---

*"A Refusal to Mourn the Death, by Fire, of Child in London."

is an expensive limited edition, beautifully done. Lax you would like. I have read the Bouyer book, or part of it, and it is very fine. I am interested in Protestantism now, am having some meetings with Protestant theologians, pleasant, honest and earnest men: but how serious are they I wonder. No more than Catholic theologians of the same temper and background.

What I am going to do now is send you a manuscript of a recent thing of mine, which might interest you: *Notes on a Philosophy of Solitude.* I do not say it represents anything much but it is my own authentic voice of the moment and it has had a hard time with the censors of the Order. And here is a poem too: optimistic I suppose but it is an optimistic-*néant.* But you see, for me emptiness is fullness, not mere vacuum. But in tribute to the seriousness of this happy void I ought to make it more empty and not be so quick to say positive things about it. This I agree.

I like *Dissent* when I can get it. I will look up the winter issue. Here in Kentucky such wild magazines come rarely. Tell Herbert that I liked his poems, and remember me to Alpha. And express to Mme Weil my admiration for Simone, on principle at least, for I have yet to give her a direct and thoughtful reading.

I do not know if Curtis Brown is helping you much. Naomi Burton has left them, and with her gone it is just a matter of business as far as I am concerned. I am thinking seriously of leaving them. I am very eager to see your book. When will it appear in French? And, by the way, would you please send me a couple of issues of *Kultura* with my "Letter to the Innocent Bystander" in it—I can always give it to one or two university libraries which like to collect all my stuff.

I enjoy writing to you and hearing from you in return, and believe that it is very important for both of us to correspond like this, not with any arrière pensée connected with the Church, for such baldly external ways of considering spiritual things are not meaningful to me. Friendship is the first and most important thing, and is the true cement of the Church built by Christ. I am solitary enough to value any genuine contact highly, and I assure you I have not very many. There are only very few in the monastery to whom I can talk as I talk to you: there is one only here, and he has very little to say in reply, he just listens, because he came here young and knows nothing. But he listens intelligently. I value the sound of your voice and appreciate highly anything that you say. Now I must end this long letter, in order to get it started on its way to France. God bless you always—

> With very cordial friendship in Christ
> Tom Merton

I am sending the poem herewith and the article under separate cover by sea mail.

A Message from the Horizon

Look, a naked runner,
A messenger,
Following the wind
From budding hills.

By sweet sunstroke
Wounded and signed
(He is therefore sacred)
Silence is his way.

Rain is his own
Most private weather.
But surprise is his first star.

This stranger, this
Early hope flies fast:
A mute comet, an empty sun:
Adam is his name!

O primeval angel
Virgin brother of astonishment,
Born of one word, one bare
Inquisitive diamond!

O blessed
Invulnerable cry,

O unplanned Saturday!
O lucky Father!

Come without warning
O friend of hurricanes,
Lightning in your bones!
We will open to you
Our most noble door:

Open to rain, to somersaulting air,
To everything that swims,
To skies that wake
Flare and applaud!

    (It is too late: he flew the other way,
    Wrapping his honesty in rain!)

*** *** ***

Pardon all runners
All speechless, alien winds,
All mad waters.

Pardon their impulses
Their wild attitudes
Their young flight—their reticence!

When a message has no clothes on
How can it be spoken?

Pornic, July 8, 1960

Dear Merton,

1. You should not call yourself a bourgeois. First, if that term can be used in social sciences, one should be careful in applying it to Mr. X or Mr. Y, as we encounter here a thorny problem of the typical, so thorny that Marxists have been unable to cope with it. Second, for the last ten years I have been living in France and only here the term has a very palpable meaning, even of a dream of the people: "maison bourgeoise", "ma bourgeoise". Every country is difficult to bear, France has some horrifying features of its own. Here in Pornic (Loire Atlantique) I feel again a wave of disgust mounting. This power of money—for generations, as French bourgeoisie is several centuries old—transforming and poisoning all human relationships. You complain about Americans and you are not wrong but it seems to me power of money is greater in France, more subterranean, penetrating every tissue, only negative, in the form of fear, of miserliness, of just sitting on the riches agglomerated by ancestors. Those villas along the coast, those big apartments in Paris, empty for the greatest part of the year, cupboards, chest drawers full of goods of all kinds etc. I think of a Polish friend of mine who teaches German in a Catholic lycée in Bordeaux (François Mauriac's lycée) and earns 50 dollars

[79]

per month. I think also of all the African Negroes, Arabs, Indo-Chinese whose sweat and misery went into those villas, houses, cupboards. To earn a decent living is very hard in this country if not impossible and I would have been in a bad shape had I to rely upon monies earned in France. That French intellectuals issued from those families who were heaping riches for centuries develop a "mauvaise conscience" is natural but je me méfie, I believe their revolt is false, to put it brutally, it is perhaps just a masked search for new security, in the best tradition of their predecessors. Sartre is publishing now a series of articles on Cuba in— astonishingly enough—*France-Soir*. It looks honest and correct—but I am sure it is not: too neat, too logical—revolutions are never so neat and problems of any country are usually much more involved than observers from outside believe. And they are all like that, French intellectuals. They are running around the world looking for a pure, ideal revolution. Une idée de la révolution. Of course, I had my complexes too. I have never belonged to bourgeoisie, for the simple reason that it was practically inexistent in Poland. I come from a country gentry, in the second generation, as my father belonged already to landless intelligentsia. Probably the revolution in Poland and my service with the government of "people's democracy" cured me from "origine complexes". I am class or group or caste-conscious—of belonging to the intellectual caste. You belong to it too, sociologically speaking, even if the role of that group is less defined in America.

2. Thank you for "Notes for a philosophy of solitude." I have read the manuscript with profit. Simone Weil says that mystical life is governed by strict laws and reality of that life is confirmed by writings of contemplatives of various religions who always speak of the same experience and even their effort of grasping it in words is identical. Every reader of your manuscript must put to himself the question: whether he is up to exigencies enumerated. So I was putting to myself that question, this is unavoidable. My answer is negative. I cannot afford too great interiorisation and have to keep myself on the level defined by *The Cloud of Unknowing* as contemplation of one's own wretchedness. There is the element time—and meditation on time throws us back to the story of our life, where I discover first of all wounds of ambition, self-love, an attempt to find compensations (literature:), so emptiness—which is the core of the matter—is for me unattainable. And I feel myself as a disgusting heap of meat, of fat and of bones, imprisoned as I am in my "I". My revolt has been largely individualistic only, which is bad. Some other, better impulses were mixed with it. I hope I learned something those last years through writing in order to be

useful, for instance by translating Simone Weil into Polish etc. But this is not going into a desert, ambition plays its role too. I have had not long ago a conversation with one of the Polish bishops who came to Paris. I liked him, a fat man with eyes petillants d'intelligence. He told me he knew that book of Simone Weil's texts nearly by heart and has been using it in all his sermons. That was for me what is called "gratte-menton". So my activity is socially determined and I cannot claim solitude. But without a certain amount of solitude and without texts of contemplatives I become very soon sterile.

3. In June I was in West Berlin where I attended the meeting of the Congress for Cultural Freedom. There were several people from India and listening to them I came to conclusions unfavorable to the future of their civilisation. No bread will be made out of that flour. What they take for a spiritual vocation of their tradition is probably a lack of rigorous thinking only. There is a dreamy quality in their vague aspirations towards a syncretic, all-embracing religion, universal goodness, rational social system—a curious blend of Anglo-Saxon empiricism with oriental un-shape. The best among the Americans were Robert Oppenheimer and George Kennan. As I noticed Oppenheimer is under the influence of Simone Weil—it is astonishing to what extent that girl is fructuating. A tendency of Oppenheimer to quote Hindu texts I found a bit disquieting. I have been told it

was because Oppenheimer started his studies by two years of Sanscrit, so he had to make use of that knowledge sometimes. Perhaps.

You know that I am sceptical about Russia—in spite of Boris Pasternak. What Russia *is* no Westerner knows—only some Russians and some Poles do. I am sceptical about China and India—in terms of the yeast in the remote future. As to America, I do not know. Anglo-Saxons are protected against many follies by their reluctance to grasp any philosophy of history—that reluctance is at the same time their weakest point.

4. I decided to dig into our roots, namely the period of "fin-de-siècle." I am reading a great Polish writer, always misunderstood in his native country and forgotten (for political reasons), while completely unknown abroad: Stanislaw Brzozowski, who died in 1912 at the age of 33. And I am making discoveries: we have been turning round in the XXth c. All the problems which interest now neo-Marxists, existentialists-Marxists etc. have been posed long ago. If Brzozowski was misunderstood, that was because his thought for his contemporaries was just incoherent: Hegel, philosophy of history, Marxism, Christianity (striking analogies with utterances of Yuri's uncle in *Doctor Zhivago*). But his thought was coherent and vigorous. Difficult—much easier now, fifty years after his death. I tell you this as it is connected with our discussion on Nature. Brzozowski was

raving against philosophy of the second half of the XIXth c., in his opinion Marxism was the peak of "aboutissement" of European philosophy, but he applied what is called today existentialist analysis to the human situation of Hegel and of Marx and saw in them an inevitable flaw resulting from a scientistic image of Nature as an external necessity. The whole evolutionist image of the "iron laws" of Nature was for him an outcome of social processes, of a romantic "de-doublement" into the external world which crushes us and our "internal life" incapable to shape the world—so Marx-ists projected iron laws of Nature into Society and the trans-formation of the world had to come according to them "externally", through (providential?) processes. Forgive me those involved sentences which cannot render the real sense. In any case I thought when reading Brzozowski that perhaps you, rejecting or not feeling "iron cruelty" of Nature, were not completely wrong, that we all are perhaps too much influenced by that most demoniac science, biology. Notice that Simone Weil is on the opposite pole than you: for her everything was Necessity and Grace operated so to say through what seems to us a pure impossibility and contra-diction.

As to myself, I have always felt the burden of blind and cruel necessity, of mechanism, in Nature, in my body, in my psychology. For me History, as a purely human domain, alien to Nature, meant liberation. In Marxism there are mixed elements, dialectical (freedom, humanity as opposed to Nature or what man imagines Nature is) and materialistic (self-regulating processes external to the will of man). It is curious to note that Polish "revisionists" (Brzozowski was one already) are dialecticians, while Stalinists are materialists.

5. Alpha spent several months in Paris. Quite success abroad—his books are being translated into several languages, helped also by the renown of his film *Ashes and diamonds* (a good film). One novel of his appeared already in English: *Torquemada* in Britain, perhaps *Inquisitors* in America. On Inquisition (in fact on Communist New Faith). Also *Les Portes du Paradis* in Sartre's *Temps Modernes*.* We are cordial friends. Fundamental discussions difficult. "I was stupid, that's all"—this does not advance the argument. He is quite impossible when drunk—his immesurable ambition bursts up then. Do not believe I am not a drunkard too, sometimes. Of late I feel an urge to drink and to talk—when you are near 50 that's a critical age. I realised that we do not change—that was the most important lesson from our talks. He is frail, weak, interested only in his private life, his family (he has two children), his homosexual love affairs, and that was always so—political

* *The Inquisitors*, translated by Konrad Syrop, 1960. Andrzejewski's *Les Portes du Paradis*, translated by J. Lisowski, appeared in *Les Temps Modernes*, October 1960. It was published in England as *The Gates of Paradise*, translated by James Kirkup, 1963.

attitudes have never been for him au fond important. I reproached him that he is throwing out the baby with the bath, after he had lost his Communist faith and represents just a complete scepticism. He agreed. Taken together, those contacts gave me a feeling of brotherhood in weakness, in frailty, though in the beginning I had a tendency to sermonize, of which soon I became ashamed.

Herbert left for Poland this Spring. I have had a letter from him, very sad. After 2 years spent in France he has difficulty to readapt himself to not too brilliant conditions. On the border, they had confiscated several books he was carrying, among others my new book. As to his poems, I thank you for your offer. They are deposed with *Encounter* in London, which wants to print them—if I learn that they do not publish them, I will let you know.

6. Translations of my new book are lagging. Probably the German and Italian ones will appear first. With French translation many misfortunes. Bargainings with Gallimard, who always pays too little. No English language publisher. Curtis Brown presented the book to Doubleday who rejected it based upon a report which doubted whether there is enough public eager to read about such internally European affairs. I am in touch with two other publishers but not through Curtis Brown and I do not know really whether I should pay him 10 percent in case I conclude an agreement.

7. You are right when you say you should not write against "the world" in general etc. But we are in a bad fix: the present state of affairs is so complicated that in order to understand the main forces of evil active today, one has to plunge deep into socio-philosophical studies. And nobody understands—neither in the West nor in the East. Everything which is valid turns around Marxism—not Marxism itself but its philosophical byproducts. A magazine *Soviet Survey* published in London can be of use to you, especially the April–June 1960 issue on revisionism. Also *Dissent.* It seems to me that your role in America is determined by the following factors: (a) a nostalgia to get out of the "rat's race", a sort of revolt against values accepted by a commercial civilisation, the proof of which are beatniks, buddhism, Zen etc.; (b) intellectual and moral weakness of American Christian churches; (c) chaos in the world of literary and artistic values. I wonder whether you could not be useful as a guide to many people who look for something blindly if you take things by a bias, for instance of literary criticism. Years of monastery prepare for such a task. Literature shows many phenomena of which people who write it are most often not conscious. Our XIXth c. poet, Norwid,* used to say that poetry is no more than a percentage from contem-

*Cyprian Norwid (1821–83), Polish poet whose sense of irony and preoccupation with the questions of history have had a strong influence on twentieth-century Polish poets.

plation, the same applies to literary criticism. Such a task would be primarily a negative one, through rejection of many values taken for granted by poets, novelists etc. too, but also a positive one thanks to clarification. I pull you to my side, of useful activity, but if you write, by a mere fact of writing you are not out of the world and we should well choose the neuralgic points for our attack.

8. I have received two offers to come as a visiting lecturer on Polish literature to America. I rejected the offer from Bloomington, Indiana (Indiana University). Pity, Bloomington is near Kentucky. I was tied by my promise given to the University of California (Berkeley), besides California university is more interesting. The matters stand now as follows: by principle I agreed, but there are questions of travel expenses of my family and I do not know whether and when everything will be ready—whether this coming academic year. I feel some temptations to teach, perhaps I am right, perhaps I am wrong.

Your letters—I answer them after a long delay not to overburden you with so to say extra-mural preoccupations. Often I have a desire to answer immediately, but perhaps it is better to wait and let the time go on.

Cordially
Czeslaw Milosz

Czeslaw Milosz   Oct. 30, 1960
2601 Ridge Road
Berkeley 9, Cal.

Dear Merton,

A few weeks ago I came with my family to Berkeley where I teach Polish literature. Quite a turmoil those last months, changing plans etc. I have had another proposal, from the University of Indiana. Bloomington has the advantage of being situated near Kentucky and near Merton, but California had approached me earlier and I am here.

I left the United States exactly 10 years ago and this return forces me to look back at those years. My decision then—to go to Europe and to stick, if possible, to Poland—was rationally speaking foolish but, as I see today, necessary. Staying in America I would have not done in all probability what I succeeded to do; sufferings and European political nervousness pushed and prodded me. My state of mind is that of a great gratitude to God for everything, for many miraculous happenings and narrow escapes.

Ten years ago I just escaped from America, being afraid of life without purpose and of acedia.* I did not find in America then anything to which I could be committed. I

---

*Acedia is one of the seven cardinal sins. In his essay "Saligia," Milosz defines it as "terror in the face of emptiness, apathy, depression" (*Beginning with My Streets*).

had few illusions about Poland and less even after my stay in Warsaw in 1950, but after I found a refuge in France I elaborated slowly a "way of life" committed to writing and publishing in Polish. Now I question myself and do not know as yet whether I learned enough to face America, or to be more exact, moral problems connected with living in America. Or rather one problem: whether it is possible to preserve, to create if you prefer, a clear purpose of one's activity. By America I mean this modern Western civilisation—while when in France I was leading a life of an alien, in a double sense alien: as un intellectuel de gauche who scoffs at political absurdities of France, as a Pole who just shrugs his shoulders at many aberrations of French intellectuals. I do not think such aloofness is possible or indicated here, unless one is ready to retreat into academism. At the present moment I am groping towards first blueprints of my literary activity, no more. "Literary" is incorrect as I have to read much and to meditate before I find something. What I feel is a sort of big confrontation which I eluded until now or perhaps postponed. And not only my personal confrontation, also more universal, in any case for a certain type of people. We (to designate that group by "we") take more or less for granted that "alienation" (in a sociological, early-Marxist sense) of man in a capitalist society which is at the core (if one looks more attentively) of our revolts. On the other hand, the belief in a society free of "alienation" (socialist etc) is dead. But a basic impulse, an attitude having its roots in romanticism, a hostility towards life consisting in earning and spending, in "just living", remains vivid. All this—if you permit a jump, a raccourci of thought—can be reduced to the question of relationship between History and human nature. Besides, for many years it has been a central problem of my meditations. Two extremes: a complete historical fluidity and human nature dissolved in it (which nourishes Marxist dreams of "transformation of man") versus stability of "natural laws" (this element strong in America inherited from le siècle des Lumières, also strong, for other and more deep reasons, in Catholicism and an ally of Church conservatism). Jacques Maritain* in his *Reflexions sur l'Amérique* touched upon a very vital point of hatred of European intellectuals for America (he quotes *The Plumed Serpent* of Lawrence but indeed it is a real passion of practically all European intellectuals—I observed that for years). And he is right explaining this by a thwarted religious urge.

To put it another way: since there is a danger in living here—a danger of accepting life as it is, of taking rules of a

*Jacques Maritain (1882–1973), philosopher and a preeminent interpreter of Thomas Aquinas. In his monumental *Creative Intuition in Art and Poetry* (1953), Maritain argues that human art continues the labor of divine creation and warns against "pure art," devoid of human or natural context, as a sterile enterprise. In *The Captive Mind*, Milosz notes that Maritain was despised by Communists as degenerate.

given society for immutable, for "natural laws", of grazing like a cow, I suppose a possible cure can consist in turning that danger into a subject of reflection, through a sort of dialectical turn. Yet one can lose. Perhaps I overestimate my resources. That field is very vast—it stretches from theology to social thought of the XIXth c. I try to arm myself in advance against possible complications resulting from my coming here for a visiting lectureship. There are already hints at the university as to my staying as a professor. In making decisions I cannot take into account my person only, as I have two children (boys of 9 and 13) and it is hard to condemn them to a life of permanent instability as in France where they shared my status (and a legal status) of a refugee.

It happened so that we live just two steps from the Berkeley Newman Hall. I read Catholic publications with much more interest than any others. It seems to me many things are going on in America, there is a change. Paris perspective is false to the extent it does not reach further than politics (for instance articles on Cuba amazing by their superficiality and very similar to what Paris press published about Poland—until after 1956 practically all proved to be a lie). Oh, that desire of Paris intellectuals to find some place a "pure" revolution! A desire stemming from the same root as their hatred of America as a society which established itself in the imperfect.

I have to read thological books. I have been preparing myself through Simone Weil and I need it. In 1950, in Warsaw, I said to a friend of mine, "In ten years I shall write on God, but not earlier". Perhaps by "writing" I meant pronouncing His name. A detour, a long detour, is necessary—I ask myself whether I am a victim of my illusions when I think that perhaps I can touch upon theology without falling into a denial of "historicité" or a kind of immobilism.

My last book, *Europe Natale* has not had until now much chance in America, Curtis Brown does not seem efficient. An Italian translation will appear shortly, a German will follow this season, Gallimard is my publisher in France but he looks now for a translator. Of late I published a small book on Hungary, in Polish, consisting of my introduction and my translations, not from the Hungarian (I do not know that difficult language) but through a French version: an essay on history of Hungary, an essay on the policy of the Hungarian Communist Party 1945–1956 (written in Budapest by an ex-Party member after the uprising of 1956) and some poems of young Hungarian poets.

You can help and guide me. I hope to meet you personally one day. I had some scruples as to our correspondence— I did not want to take too much of your time for answers. But now your letter would be for me a great joy. Perhaps you know somebody in Berkeley whom I should meet. I am meeting people here but on a rather superficial level of parties. Perhaps you could suggest magazines I do not know. I find *The Critic* quite good, i.e. in harmony with its limited purpose.

With love
Czeslaw Milosz

✳

Nov. 9, 1960

My Dear Milosz:

It was a great pleasure to get your letter of Oct. 30th and to realize that you were actually in America. In your earlier letter you spoke of coming to Berkeley but I did not realize that your plans were so definite. It is a pity in one sense that you did not come to Bloomington, but certainly Berkeley will be much better for you, and San Francisco is one of the few cities in this country with a character of its own and some culture. I should think that if things go well you would be wise to stay.

Certainly there are enormous problems and difficulties about the life of an intellectual in America. There is the awful shame and revolt at being in this continual milkshake, of being a passive, inert captive of Calypso's Island where no one is ever tempted to think and where one just eats and exists and supports the supermarket and the drug store and

General Motors and the TV. Above all there is the shame, the weakness which makes us hesitate to associate ourselves with what has become the object of universal scorn and hate on the part of the intellectuals in Europe. But since courage is the first thing, maybe we need courage to dissociate ourselves from our own tribe and its conventions, which are just a little more subtle, a little differently poisonous, from the obvious depravation of the lotus eaters. In reality I think you will find here many healthy unexploited possibilities. There are fine and honest people who really do seek honest answers and ask to be *led* by someone. God knows, no one with any sense wants to command an army of intellectual lotus eaters. And in the end one gets the feeling that as soon as anything gets serious they will drop off and vanish into the undergrowth. One feels these people coming at one with childlike good will, sincere curiosity, and no depth, no earnestness except in pretense. They *seem* to want something, in fact to want everything. But to want everything is in fact to want nothing. One has to specify, otherwise choices are of no significance: they are not choices.

Then in the background are the army high command and the captains of industry. These are the serious birds, and theirs is another kind of seriousness altogether, because they are definitely not fooling. The intellectuals, perhaps, are. The brass hats don't know exactly what they want, but they almost know: and it is negative. They are getting tired of being hated and want to give the world a genuine reason for hating them. No doubt they will. Theirs is a pragmatic, unspoken pride which is all the deeper and more incurable for being unspoken. It speaks with its effects, for which no one claims either honor or responsibility but they are devastating and inescapable.

So I am tempted to wonder whether you and I do not after all have some kind of responsibility toward these people who are certainly, up to a point, waiting for anything we say, and quite ready to accept it. I fear being deluded and deceived by them. Perhaps I fear it too much and this may have a lot to do with my solitude, which always anticipates defeat and frustration. But after all if we have a hearing, we ought to humbly and courageously say what we have to say, clearly, forcefully, insistently and for the glory of God's truth, not for any self-interest. And of course this means that we will *not* be pure, either. But knowing we will partly fail, we can at least try to be, and accept the consequences.

You are certainly right that the European intellectuals are guilt-ridden fools trying to go on believing in the perfect revolution somewhere. Certainly you should give it a good year, and have your say, and continue to think and meditate and read. I am sure you are on the threshold of a new development that is very important, and I am equally sure that it is better for you to be here than in France right now, though it may not be apparent just why. Simone Weil has been very good for you. I am glad you are optimistic about the Catholic thinkers and writers in this country. There is a very good Catholic poet at Oakland, a Dominican Brother, Brother Antoninus,* who also is a printer. Get in touch with him and say that I suggested you come to see him. I think he might be able to introduce you to some interesting people. He knows the writers in San Francisco anyway. I also suggest you go on down the coast to Monterrey and Big Sur and see the Camaldolese hermitage, though this is really nothing. Just a few old hermits and some kids in shacks, but a wild, beautiful place. You can find a kind of refuge there, to think and read. There are of course a lot of writers, mostly beats, at Big Sur. People out there can tell you about it.

Have you sent your book to Farrar, Straus and Cudahy? Bob Giroux is my friend and editor there. He might like the book. A Catholic publisher might take it, too. Sheed and Ward, or Regnery. By the way, do you know that I have never seen *Europe Natale*? I want very much to read it. Can you send me a copy? Or shall I write to France to get it. I am not sure whether I sent you my own *Disputed Questions*. The book came out just about when you must have been coming over here and maybe it got lost in the shuffle. I am sending you another copy in a few days. I will also send you some copies of

*Brother Antoninus, or William Everson (1912–94), a monk and poet who became associated with the Beat poets of San Francisco.

the magazine *Jubilee*, which is very good in its way, and run by good friends of mine. It would be wonderful if you did something for them, though they don't pay very much.

I know *Dissent*, and get it when I can: but that is always a bit uncertain out in this part of the country. I like it very much. I will try to get the other one you mention.

You gave me some very good suggestions in the other letter. Especially about the oblique approach, through literary criticism. I might do that, or better go at it through creative writing. I am also doing some abstract drawings at the moment. Other avenues will open up to me I am sure. Pious literature is not going to go very far, but more reflective and more fundamental things can be expressed in a variety of ways.

I would like very much to get Alpha's *Inquisition* and wish you would tell me the publisher. I think often of him and pray for him. There is no use in our being upset by weakness and sin in anyone: we are all in the same boat, and there is no point in being squeamish and repelled by it. On the contrary, as you say, it is good to feel one has companions in weakness: this can be the most healthy approach. I have certainly not come to the monastery to feel myself isolated from sin, but to bear all sins along with my own and to be, as Dostoevsky's Zossima says, responsible to everyone for everything. It is not exactly charming, and it is sometimes like being in hell.

You are very right to have no further confidence in and nothing further to do with Curtis Brown. They are useless.

I shall tell J. Laughlin* of New Directions to see you when he is out there, he will certainly be interested in some Polish poets etc. He is a good sort and will give you many leads and good connections.

I have received full permission to see you any time you come this way. I hope you will come. Always be sure to let me know in plenty of time. I am very happy that you are "here" (though almost as far away as in France). Thanks again for your letters. They are a great encouragement to me, our problems are very alike, in the professional and intellectual field at any rate.

God bless you always, and your family.

Very cordially yours in Christ
Tom Merton

*James Laughlin (1914–) founded New Directions in 1936, specializing in avant-garde and experimental authors and works, among them Henry Miller, Ezra Pound, and William Carlos Williams.

Dear Merton,

I have read with astonishment your article on Heraclitus (or Herakleitos, as you justly spell) and your translations.* This is for me a proof of our deep spiritual affinity—if I dare to use that expression. I ended my book of essays published in 1958 (in Polish only) by those fragments.† I have written also a poem on Heraclitus. It seems to me you are right when you stress "intuition pre-chrétienne" of Heraclitus. Also Marxists are right when they stress another side (or the same?) of Heraclitean philosophy. And Boris Pasternak for instance tried to grasp both sides. In Heraclitus there is the thought of the future, of our common future, true dialectic as opposed to the false one. As to his Fire, among many meanings I remember what Oscar Milosz said about "incorporeal light" as the first stage of Creation, in accordance with "medieval schools of Oxford and of Chartres".

If I said good things on the Catholic press in America, it was because I see in it a sense of purpose, of useful activity as contrasted with a madhouse. My impression here is that of a man confronted with a social body stricken by

* The Behavior of Titans.

† Milosz wrote his poem "Heraclitus" in Montgeron in 1960. It appeared in *King Popiel and Other Poems*, 1962. Milosz's interest in Heraclitus dates from his high-school years, when he wrote an examination essay on Heraclitus' river of time, a figure which persists in his poetry.

a heavy, perhaps mortal, illness. Anti-communism fed to the Americans is based on completely false premises as they do not realise to what extent they are deprived of freedom. They do not know and in consequence do not understand what happens in the world. People in Poland are extremely sceptical as to the press controlled by the government but they receive ten times more information than people here and commentaries are, in spite of the Party line, much more honest. I feel the heavy illness of American society is closely connected with "mass media", one should look for its roots there. No social body can be so basically anti-Heraclitean without incurring punishment. In spite of all the distortions there is in communism a Heraclitean element, it is alive and all the revolts within Marxism are in the name of that element. People in America have the road to that element completely barred. Consequences are enormous.

I write this after our return from Los Gatos, a small town south of San Francisco where we spent a couple of days with my colleague from the high school, who is teaching astrophysics at the Jesuit University of Santa Clara. My children were looking for hours at television, to my impotent rage. This is a great responsibility to expose one's children to such influences—most often imperceptible to them—and to make decisions, as my decision of coming here, which risk distorting their lives. Just a few minutes before the television for me were enough to induce a state of shame and sadness for the whole evening. Among other nice things—commercials humiliating for human beings engaged in them—I saw the face of a judge from the South who proclaimed that desegregation is "communism": imagine those Negroes who listened to him and the only kind of conclusion they could come to.

It seems to me that America is bursting with talents and intelligence, but minds are turning round in a sort of spellbound dance of paralytics. The awakening is inevitable—but when and what awakening? As to myself I know I can disintegrate completely if I do not keep my thinking clear and hot. So I have started a sort of diary exactly on those problems—of confrontation.

What is needed is not the language of neurotics, of "lotus eaters", psychological subtleties addicts. Things should be called by their name. This structure, this system is not livable. Perhaps a great mistake of Catholics consists in this: they are satisfied too much with the notion of "human nature" and there is no place in their thinking for what is neither the individual nor society but society established in the soul of the individual. Perhaps a few individuals can liberate themselves under the influence of Grace. But millions and millions are condemned to terrible limitations which are not their fault.

Is not that a weak point of Thomistic philosophy? Is not so that a pioneering task in this respect is being done by Marxists—or, as now, by existential-Marxists who return to the early writings of Marx when he was not yet an economist (he started with studies of alienation and discovered the Proletariat later).

I am in correspondence with a young Polish Marxist who has published of late an interesting book on history of Russian thought in the XIXth c. We missed each other just by a day—he was here in Berkeley, now he is for a few months in England, before his return to Poland. He agrees with me that the problem of alienation is basically theological. He says: "Marxism contains religious elements, this does not shock me, on the contrary, I rejoice. The question of alienation, the existentialist question, is the religious heart of Marxism. Our group in Warsaw is a sort of religious sect." He means by their group a circle of young Marxist philosophers looked askance at by the Party and labelled "revisionist". All my sympathies go to that group.

I have been and I am, as you probably guess, rongé par ma culpabilité. Especially by some of my books. Perhaps I should not have written them, especially *The Captive Mind*—as I understood more then what was put into that book. The harm done to readers in Poland is lesser, as they know others writings of mine, as well as circumstances, and are able to place that book in context. But foreign readers?

Did not I contribute to the cold war, instead of presenting those dilemmas on a more serious, philosophical level?

Of course I am confronted with the subject "America and I". I do not believe I could "adapt myself" in the sense of choosing this society, here, as an object of my activity. All my thoughts and my reactions are determined by another society, Polish, which has a revolution already behind it. And when writing I think of that other society, which is the indispensable condition for me of moving forward—while if I could write for American periodicals it would be just a vulgarisation of thoughts proceeding in Polish by short-cuts. It is possible that I am guilty of having left Poland, guilty towards my own possibilities and gifts. Perhaps I paralysed myself in that way. But I have to make use of a given situation, the best I can.

American intellectuals seem to me completely lost in impotent negation. The case of Norman Mailer arrested in New York because he had stabbed his wife takes on symbolic dimensions. What would be needed is a hierarchy of aims—aims for an attack. Before any political action is possible the start should be made by what makes any serious political and intellectual action impossible, i.e. "mass media".

I have an idea, perhaps crazy. To tell the truth you are probably the only man in America who can start a big and serious action. The way of proceeding is as follows. You receive permission to look at television for a week. Then you write an appeal to all the people who are fed up with that stultifying enterprise of commercial firms. They are numerous. You ask for a campaign with clear objectives: 1. All the television stations should be nationalized* along the British pattern—like the BBC. 2. A special body composed of scholars, writers, clergymen should be created to act as a direction. 3. No commercials should be permitted (and they are the true cause of idiocy). Time on television will be allotted to all the organizations, churches, foundations etc. recognized as of public interest (there is a trap here: if time is sold at exorbitant prices, television will be used by powerful money interests, but certainly one can conceive means of avoiding that danger).

If you secure the backing of some circles of the Catholic church and if you launch such an appeal, you will fail at first. Yet your appeal will provoke a great stir. It will be a sign of breaking the generalised apathia and impotence. A sign of your belief in personal responsibility which always incites people to be aware of their own responsibility. And, since nationalisation (a word terrifying in this country) of television and of radio is inevitable anyway—sooner or later—the honor of being in the vanguard will belong to American Catholics thanks to your initiative.

Intellectuals have been discussing for years the evils of

*Vide P.S. [Milosz's note]

"mass communications" but they proceeded like naturalists describing a phenomenon completely beyond the power of man. Yet the phenomenon is not as mysterious as they try to convince us. Experience shows that in those countries where television is non-commercial, the news coverage is good, much, much better than here, and the television is the domain of serious writers, actors, singers etc. In Great Britain, under the pressure of British neo-capitalism, a parallel, commercial, television was introduced. It is preferred by many: and here we encounter the most thorny problem of democracy—if in every man is a sage and an idiot, whoever flatters the idiot wins.

But I do not incite you to win at once. This issue should be presented as having a solution, not as a theme of intellectual wailings. A growing movement of awareness can be tranformed, could take on the form of a loose organization, for instance by a pledge to boycott television as it is now. Personally, I can protest only in that way, by refusing to buy a television set, in spite of pressures on the part of my children (in my elder son's school only 5 or 6 children have no sets at home).

Crazy. Every sober person would tell you that in the existing system of economy and of politics there is no slightest chance to succeed. Perhaps. But no politician, no intellectual would raise that issue—much less because of hopelessness, much more because he would be afraid of being accused politically—of socialism, communism etc. A Trappist monk is beyond such suspicions. He can invoke his real care—the human soul debased every day in an imperceptible (for that soul) way.

Pardon me if you find I am dreaming. It is difficult to live without asking ourselves: "What can be done?" Impotence is dangerous. That's why I am so jumpy.

I am sending you a clipping from *Le Monde* concerning Alpha (Jerzy Andrzejewski)*. The broadcast in question was recorded a year ago, before Jerzy came to Paris, and now just repeated on the radio—he spoke about his souvenirs of wartime. He is in a difficult position financially—for ideological reasons the ministry did not give him permission to sell the film rights to his work *Les Portes du Paradis* (on the Children's Crusade) published by *Les Temps Modernes* de Sartre. But after all this is Poland where always "on s'arrange". I received news from him—he had gotten a weekly chronicle with another periodical.

> with love
> Czeslaw Milosz

P.S. My book *Europe Natale* has not been published as yet by Gallimard. I imagine they are translating it, it is not ready.

*Some details in that clipping are mixed up. [Milosz's note]

P.S. If I put that word "rationalization", it is because to be against the existing state of affairs is not enough. Of course, not necessarily state ownership, it would be enough to transfer control to any institutions of "public interest". Neither the very proposal is important: only a feeling given to people that we deal with problems which *can* be solved by man, that society is not omnipotent and we are not condemned to be passive tools or (innocent) witnesses.

But please, treat everything I wrote on television just as an outburst of indignation. Emotionality.

March 28, 1961

Dear Milosz:

It is a terribly long time since your last letter. And it was a good one too. The better they are, the longer I wait to answer them, because I am always hoping for a chance to really think about everything you say and really answer it. Because it is true that what you say affects me deeply, seeing that we are in many respects very much alike. Consequently any answer must involve the deepest in me, and that is not easy. We always seek to evade the expression of what is most important to us, in fact we are usually not able even to confront it. Haste gives us the opportunity to substitute something else for the deepest statements.

I am very glad you came to America, and have seen everything close at hand. You are all too right about the sickness of this society. It is terrible and seems to get worse. I feel nothing but helplessness in my situation: I should ideally speaking have a wonderful perspective from which to see things in a different—a Heraclitean—light. But at the same time there is so much confusion around me and in my own self. In monastic life there is a fatal mixture of inspiration and inertia that produces an awful inarticulate guilt in anyone who does not simply bury his head in the sand. You never know when you are right and how far you can go in studying the world outside and reacting to it. There are infinite temptations, the first of which is to think that one is separate from it all and somehow "pure", while really we are full of the same poisons. Hence we fight in ourselves many of the same ambiguities. There is always the temptation to justify ourselves by condemning "the world". You are perfectly right about the "spellbound dance of paralytics". You are right too that they anaesthetize themselves with the double talk of lotus eaters, the psychological talk: all this talk about responsibility and personalism and organization men and whatnot tends to be a part of the spell and of the dance. What is behind it? The obsession with concepts, with knowledge, with techniques, as if we were supposed to be able to manipulate everything. We have got ourselves into a complete fog of concepts and "answers". Illusory answers to illusory problems and never facing the real problem: that we have all become zombies.

This works on several levels, of course. It is quite obvious on the level of the race fanatics, but on the intellectual level it persists too. I think the Marxist psychology of bourgeois individualism is not too far wrong when it condemns the perpetual turning around and around in circles of guilt and self-analysis: as if this were capable of doing something, or exorcising the real guilt . . . But they are in the same boat themselves, only a few stages farther back. They haven't yet got to the stage of idleness and surfeiting that will permit them to do the same thing. The poison is exactly the alienation you speak of, and it is not the individual, not society, but what comes of being an individual helpless to liberate himself from the images that society fills him with. It is a very fine picture of hell sometimes. When I see advertisements I want to curse they make me so sick, and I do curse them. I have never seen TV, that is never watched it. Once when I did happen to pass in front of a set I saw the commercial that was on: two little figures were dancing around worshipping a roll of toilet paper, chanting a hymn in its honor. I think this is symbolic enough, isn't it? We have simply lost the ability to see what is right in front of us: things like this need no comment. What I said above does not apply to your revisionists. I don't know much about them. I know Erich Fromm is studying along those lines. Maybe there is some hope there. If there is hope anywhere, it lies somewhere in the middle between the two extremes (which in reality meet, the extremes are closer together than the "middle" which seems to be between them).

When you say I am the only one who can start something in this country, I don't know what to say. It might ideally be true. I *should* certainly be in such a position. It should be not too difficult to give a brief, searching glance at something like TV and then really say what one has seen. In a way I would like to. Yet I realize that the position is not so simple. For one thing, I am caught by as many nets as anybody else. It is to the interests of the Order to preserve just one kind of definite image of me, and nothing else. Lately I have been expanding on all sides beyond the limits of this approved image. . . . It is not well accepted. Not that I care, but you see there would right away be very effective opposition even to so simple a matter as a study of TV and its evils. "Monks don't watch TV." And so on. For me, however, to raise this one question would mean raising an unlimited series of other questions which I am not yet prepared to face. What I would say is that if you are right, which you may be to some extent, the time is not yet ripe and I have a lot of preparing to do. I can't explain this, but I need to grow more, ripen more. My past work is nowhere near up to the level that would be required to begin something like this. My latest work is not there yet either.

Meanwhile I am going to take a vacation from writing and do a lot of reading and thinking if I can. It is really vital that I get more into the center of the real problems. I mean the real ones.

What I hope most of all is that you will be able to stop by here and that we will be able to talk. Don't worry about accommodations for your wife and children, they can be put up with friends of mine in Louisville. I do very much want to talk to you and I think it is important that we have a chance to iron out these things as it cannot be done in writing.

You are right that you would never adapt to this country. If you are out of Poland, well, you are out of it. No one knows what the future will bring. Incidentally, I don't know if I have the true picture of what is going on there but it seems to me that the flat intransigence of the Cardinal Primate* is in its own way admirable. I am not an integrist and do not want to be one, but I think the Church is right not to fool around with compromises that have no other purpose than her destruction. This at least is an honest reaction: but would that the Church reacted against the other compromises in other countries that pretend to preserve her in a way that leads only

*Stefan Wyszynski (1901–81), Archbishop of Warsaw and Primate of Poland, then under house arrest by the Soviets.

to death and to spiritual extinction, infidelity to God.

Speaking in monastic terms, of fidelity to the truth, to the light that is in us from God, that is the horror: everyone has been more or less unfaithful, and those who have seemed to be faithful have been so partially, in a way that sanctified greater evasions (the Grand Inquisitor). Perhaps the great reality of our time is this, that no one is capable of this fidelity, and all have failed in it, and that there is no hope to be looked for in any one of us. But God is faithful. It is what the Holy Week liturgy tells of His "treading the wine-press by himself". This, I think, is the central reality.

Turning back from this perspective, and looking again at the possibility of my doing something to heal the country: I don't trust myself to even begin it. There are too many ambiguities, too many hatreds, that would have to be sweated out first. I do not know if these are ever going to be sweated out in this present life. There is so much non-sense to struggle with at all times. In myself. At present I am beginning to accept this fact not with indifference but with peace and happiness because it is not as important as it seems. This, I imagine, is at least a beginning.

God bless you always. Do plan to come. Happy Easter, and bless all your family.

With all affection in Christ
Tom Merton

I forget if I sent you a *Behavior of Titans.* If you do not have it please let me know. Did you see Bro. Antoninus? I think you would like him.

※

March 28, 1961

Dear Milosz,

This is just an added note to the longer letter I mailed this morning. Don't be perturbed about *The Captive Mind.* It was something that had to be written, & apart from the circumstances, it stands as a very valid statement by itself, irrespective of how it may be read & how it may be used. In any case no matter what a writer does these days it can be "used" for the cold war or for other purposes. Our very existence can be "used" by somebody or other to "prove" something that suits him. Such things are largely meaning-less & we are wrong to be too affected by them.

The problem is your solitude. You have isolated yourself terribly by this book & hence you feel the full weight of this isolation. But you cannot seek shelter in solidarity with your Paris friends at the moment, not openly. You can do what you want to do for the time being outside of Poland—unless I am mistaken. If you were there, that also could be used for a bad purpose & its meaning twisted & vitiated.

We have to get used to our total moral isolation. It is going to get worse. We have to regain our sense of *being*, our confidence in reality, not in words. You are what you are, & what happened to the Paris writers you recorded truthfully. It happened and it has to be said. Now go on to other things, for that is already ancient history & you cannot, & need not, change it.

Bear your solitude. It is a great pain for you & there is great strength in it if you can continue to find & accept it, which you do. The torment of doubt & self-recrimination is inevitable: only do nothing to make it worse!

Again, with all blessings
Tom Merton

※

May 30, 1961

Dear Merton,

There are too many things to tell, which makes writing a letter hard. Those things are rather internal than external. Let me get rid of some details of current life first. I am going to stay here as I have been appointed a full professor and for the first time in my life I feel a "useful member of society" (I had jobs in the past but they were for me nothing but boredom). It seems to me that the best approach to such decisions is a practical one, beyond any reflexions on Europe, America etc. Here I can earn my daily bread in a honest way, that's all. As to children, intoxicated and poisoned every day by the television, I am helpless. Well, in France that was a gang of potential blousons noirs and the cinema. The parents can struggle, their will means little.

I would like to visit you in Gethsemani but I guess I should combine that trip with a trip to Madison, Wisc. Where I am invited by a school and university colleague of mine, who is a professor of Slavic Languages there. Probably during the next academic year, in the fall.

Your book *No Man Is an Island* has appeared in Poland and it has a devoted public, as I learn. It had appeared also in installments in a Catholic monthly *Znak* (*Sign*). All the problems of Polish Catholicism are extremely involved, I do not enter the subject because I would risk to write pages and pages. The atheistic campaign is in the increase. I have read a quite open proposal in one of the militant atheistic periodicals to use the term "humanism" for atheism, as it sounds more acceptable to the youth. On the other hand, a registration of Jews working in institutions which deal with abroad is going on, under pressure from Moscow. The Jews are considered a security risk.

Certainly, there is a mystery of the Jews, of their vocation. I have read Karl Stern's *The Pillar of Fire*.

I would like to talk to you and I cannot. As I said there are too many things to say. In my poetry, in my readings (except professional readings in Slavic literatures) I am pre-occupied with religious problems and I strive hard. Sometimes I think I would be an agnostic if not for my weakness. Certainly I have a tendency to a delectatio morosa, but I know a lot about myself. What is repentance? There are nights when I am oppressed by a feeling of guilt because of two or three lines of mine which seem to me artistically bad: my wounded self-love. Other nights, a remembrance of all my deeds which prove that I am inferior by nature to the vast majority of human beings: is it repentance? Or just a wounded ambition, just like in the case of not-quite-good lines? I know that "le moi est haïssable", that only renounc-ing to it one can attain purity. But I am even unable to confess: everything makes a whole of my, such and not different, nature, does not differentiate into sins. On Easter I went to confession, without profit, I feel: nothing to say, nothing to express. The Mass here in Newman Hall is a sort of gymnastics: get up, kneel, get up, sit down—like a mil-itary discipline. I impose upon myself that going to church (since 1953).

This is no subject for a letter. The situation roughly is like that: there is a certain logic of internal development. My poetry has always been religious in a deeper sense, some-times openly metaphysical, as in my long poem "The

World" written during the war. I have been praying and I know moments of great joy and harmony. To what extent is it honest? I do not intend to follow the steps of William James and other pragmatists: if it suits me, I can leave other criteria in peace. Religion rooted in our self-love, in our winding around ourselves? God inside, or our old acquaintance, our self disguised as God? My constant problem: I believe, with a part of myself (in which resides poetry and meditation on precariousness of space-time), in the Incarnation, the Resurrection and the Resurrection of the body. I cannot believe in the immortality of the soul: this is probably the greatest stumbling block for many today. It is a strange experience to have children. It incites you to utter scepticism. Heredity is our burden. We transmit it to others: shape, genes, nerves, bones and we are what our ancestors had been (original sin is perhaps easier to be grasped then).

I simplify. But those questions squeeze me more and more, especially if I consider that thousands of young people in Poland are torn between their emotional religion and the Church's teachings which do not provide them with answers understandable to them. Thomism? "Irrefutable" proofs of God's existence? Plenty. But Pascal was right when he said that a belief in God is of little use for a Christian (deists etc). I realize that nothing is more important than to find a common language with those who "search in despair", through poetry, prose, any means. Being one of them: the blind leading the lame. Yes, what is needed is a new attempt of a Pascal. Possible, in my opinion. Your books, useful as they are, do not belong to that category—Pascal engaged in a duel with Montaigne, with atheists or with himself. I see in the air the shape of such a book: somebody will write it. Perhaps you? It should be a book of great simplicity: what I believe and not why I believe but how I believe, namely, to draw a contour around what is hardly formulable, by images taken not from a religious experience*. It is probable that when one is a monk, exercise and routine transfer him so to say on the other side and certain first premises of faith become natural. But reading young Polish poetry I see there a metaphysical torment of a seriousness unknown in preceding decades—just like in films of Ingmar Bergman. I do not understand well as yet the situation in America. American Catholicism is "square" as brother Antoninus says (I like him very much, thanks for your suggestion to meet him!), perhaps the crisis is delayed here by manners and customs.

I have the choice—either to continue this letter and never to send it or send it as it is, "avec tout le baratin", I thank you for *The Wisdom of the Desert*. I did not read it as yet. Perhaps because I feel it is a sort of luxury—for those rather who coped already with some basic theological questions.

*A modern compendium, a kind of catechism. [Milosz's note]

Here is a thrust aimed at you, I do not deny. Or an appeal. By the way—you should see films of Ingmar Bergman: your monastery should see them. Forgive me: I would like to have in you an ally of the angoisse, I say what I think.

with love
Czeslaw

※

June 5th 1961.

Dear Czeslaw:

Your letter is very meaningful to me. Without having anything specific to say either I respond to it. I think we both are grasping something very important, that cannot be said. I have made too many affirmations, and while I hold to them, they do not affirm what I have intended, and they cannot. I think that I have never fully reached my final choice or stated it, and that when it comes to be stated I will end up on your side, in metaphysical torment. I have *not* coped with the basic theological questions. It only looks that way. In the depths I have more of Péguy* in me, more of Simone Weil than even I have realized, and certainly I have not let it be apparent to anyone else. There are times when I feel spiritually excommunicated. And that it is right

*Charles Péguy (1873–1914), French man of letters, who converted to Catholicism. His most famous work is *La mystère de la charité de Jeanne d'Arc.*

and honest for me to be so. It is certain that my writing is not adequate and I am oppressed by the people who think that it is and who admire it as if it really answered questions. I have given the impression I had answers.

There is something wrong with questions that are supposed to be disposed of by answers. That is the trouble with the squares. They think that when you have answers you no longer have questions. And they want the greatest possible number of answers, the smallest number of questions. The ideal is to have no more questions. Then when you have no questions you have "peace". On the other hand, the more you simply stand with the questions all sticking in your throat at once, the more you unsettle the "peace" of those who think they have swallowed all the answers. The questions cause one to be nauseated by answers. This is a healthy state, but it is not acceptable. Hence I am nauseated by answers and nauseated by optimism. There is an optimism which cheapens Christianity and makes it absurd, empties it. It is silly, petty optimism which consists in being secure because one knows the right answers.

Sometimes the answers are beautiful and obviously right. That is the great trouble, really, not that we are stopped by answers that are inadequate. The answers are in every way apparently adequate. To grasp them and hold them is to appear to be with saints and fully embodied in the community of the saints. Yet one is nauseated by them, and cast out. One is left without answers, without comfort, without companionship, without a community of saints, and in a community of people apparently confused and lost, exterior darkness. That is the thing that has finally hit me. My darkness was very tolerable when it was only dark night, something spiritually approved. But it is rapidly becoming "exterior" darkness. A nothingness in oneself into which one is pressed down further and further, until one is inferior to the entire human race and hates the inferiority. Yet clings to it as the only thing one has. Then the problem is that perhaps here in this nothingness is infinite preciousness, the presence of the God Who is not an answer, the God of Job, to Whom we must be faithful above all, beyond all. But the terrible thing is that He is *not known to others*, is incommunicable. One has no sense whatever that He is mentioned or referred to ever by anyone else, hence there is great danger that it may be the devil, for God, they say, is not at all private.

Perhaps the thing that precipitated all this was the visit to our monastery of a very good and learned monk from Europe, a scholar, full of monastic tradition, respected everywhere, an authority and quite free too from all square conventionalism. He has better answers all down the line. He has the best answers, and though I accept them intellectually something in me says "No" to them and protests against it all. I had been imagining that I could somehow fall back on these other, "better" answers. Now I see that answers are not the affair at all. The thing that shocks me is the close analogy with the workings of the Party line. The ones who "know" are actually the ones with the greatest and most detached suppleness, which is theirs because they have completely committed themselves to the cause. I could have that suppleness too if I would only yield and take a certain direction, definitively: but yield what? Let go of what?

This is what I cannot do, because it seems that if I let go in this way and gained this precious suppleness I might end up by being completely unable to say anything to you, for one, and to all those like you. And the upshot of it all is that I respect your problem, your angst, your sense of inarticulateness and inferiority a thousand times more than I respect his suppleness, his clarity, his illumination, his security. He told me I am a pessimist, and in fact he drew out all the pessimism that could possibly be latent in me by his optimism. What he was in fact telling me was not to fight. This is what I cannot not do. I will multiply negatives in honor of the God of Job.

I am really glad that you are staying in this country. Your reasons are the right ones. As for the gymnastics in the Newman Hall: there again, I sometimes wonder if there is anything else in liturgy as they conceive it self-consciously?

Would the liturgical movement solve your problem? I hope you run into it and tell me "No." To me, I admit, the gymnastic aspect of it gets in my hair but there is always a completely different dimension. There is the anger and sorrow of the psalms, not as offering answers, but as providing a voice for the essential nothingness in me that seems to be rejected, so that maybe I am not wrong about it after all. It is good after all to have prayers that are so replete with anger. The mystery of the Jews . . .

Away with the irrefutable proofs. Who needs them? I wish I could read some of the Polish poets who are struggling as you say with metaphysical dilemmas. I am convinced that this is the right atmosphere. *No Man Is an Island* is not a good book. It is too glib. I am sorry to have inflicted it on Poland. Did I send you the *Behavior of Titans**? You might like Atlas somewhat. I am going to keep quiet for a while and I do not promise to write anything like Pascal, but I am certainly bound to stop writing pious journalism. Come when you can. Fall would be a good time. October is a nice month. November can be good, but tends to be rainy.

All the best. I am glad you met and like Antoninus. God bless you, and all love.

Tom Merton

---

* *The Behavior of Titans* includes the essay on Heraclitus.

The doctrine of the immortality of the *soul* is not fully and really Christian. It is the whole person who is immortal. The whole mystery of the person. The hunger for mercy and justice survives and is fulfilled, if it be not sated in this life with too easy answers. Otherwise it has to be emptied in the next.

※

15. VI. 1961

Dear Thomas:

Just a few words to correct the impression that I am more in anguosse than I really am and that I pull you to that side. As a source of my poetry, historical meditation has a great part. There is in you a horror and attraction and solidarity with this world of history. I have been told that you had made a post-card wishing peace "in this century, the most terrible of all." But for me the XIX c. for instance was worse. I have a feeling of participating in a great movement, in a great change, deeper than political struggles but not disso-ciated from them. We are, or we can be, happier than those of the XIXth c.—think of sterile despair and irony of La-forgue. What happens is that naturalism or the view of the world as a set of "iron laws" existing *outside* of man is being overcome, that the universe is becoming *anthropocentric*—Marxism, the theory of relativity of Einstein, sociology, psychiatry work in this direction, often without being aware of it. In a sense the anthropocentric vision of Swedenborg, of William Blake too, is being rehabilitated. I am writing a study on Stanislaw Brzozowski, a Polish writer (died 1911, at the age of 32) who knew that.* Also my relative Oscar Milosz knew that, in another way. I do know that something new, a liberation of man from the slavery of naturalistic *Weltanschauung* of the XIXth., is growing. I do not agree with you when you say that you do not want answers, as answers are what the "squares" want.

They are right if they have that desire. We have to integrate new and new questions and answers into a new image of the human universe. That's why theology is, I feel, important. Even if in 99% it is frozen—read Gaston Fessard, "De l'actualité historique" where he confesses impotence of Thomism when confronted with the problem of history. Existential angst is not enough. Even films of Ingmar Bergman, an expression of that angst, are inserted into a movement, a change, as they are works of art. I feel that only a continuous chase after answers can be a driving force.

With love,
Czeslaw

*See Milosz's section on Brzozowski in *The History of Polish Literature*, 1983.

Sept. 16, 1961

Dear Czeslaw:

I wish I could write to you more often. To you I can talk, and begin to say what I want to say. Except that I cannot always begin before it is at once time to end. Anyway I do not think I sent you a copy of this Auschwitz poem,* though you may have seen it in the recent new *Beat* magazine† that City Lights Books have put out. I thought you might like this, anyway, so here it is. The *Catholic Worker* also printed it, and a sect called the Mennonites picked it up, it is getting around here and there.

Certainly I have no objections to theologians and theological thought (this refers to our last two letters back in the early summer. I only wish that theologians were more alive and that their thought was thought. Jean Daniélou was here in July and we had a couple of good conversations. He is more my style, and I get along fine with him. Yet even with him I feel there are two drawbacks: a certain reflex of ecclesiastical caution which has nothing to do with truth but only with keeping "correct" and on the right side of the authorities (to some Catholics this and this alone constitutes "truth"). The other is the fact that he writes too much and

*"Chant to Be Used in Processions around a Site with Furnaces."
†*Journal for the Protection of All Beings.*

works too much and extends it all too much, so that his thought gets spread very thin. It becomes theological journalism. Very good and sound, and alive even. But not as rich and solid as it might be. Though he is very good and a charming person.

What do you think of the international situation? I wonder if the Russians will manage to make the US population as a whole get so hysterical that they will wreck themselves, without benefit of bombs from abroad? In any case though I think there is a very real likelihood of war, and that the military on both sides are seriously thinking of one, even want it perhaps. If they get their wish, then . . . there might be something left of Argentina perhaps. I still think I will put my bet on this century as being the "worst of all". The nineteenth is gradually assuming a new shape in my mind. It was, at least in America, a very naive century. The history of the civil war is incredible. The country has never got back in touch with reality, even after two world wars. But I agree that the conquest of naturalism has been a good thing. The struggle for man to adapt himself to an anthropocentric universe is tragic: yet if he had ever really become Christian man would see and understand his present position much better. It is because men never really understood or believed in Christ that we have reached the present position. This is not a cliché, and certainly it is not meant in the sense that "men never became devout Christians." On the contrary, there have always been devout Christians, but frankly they solve no problems for anyone, least of all for the world. Christ did not die on the Cross merely so that there might be devout Christians. Incidentally I am very interested in Fromm's new presentation of the Economic and Political Mss of Marx in 1844.* It would be intriguing to really see his mind and development, if I had the time and the background. It is a bit out of my field, but anyway I read him.

There is no question in my mind that there is a need to integrate new questions and answers in a human universe: when I said I was fed up with answers, I meant square answers, ready made answers, answers that ignore the question. All clear answers tend to be of this nature today, because we are so deep in confusion and grab desperately at five thousand glimmers of seeming clarity. It is better to start with a good acceptance of the dark. That in itself contains many answers in a form that is not yet worked out: one has the answers, but not the full meaning.

Anyway here is this poem and in a few days I want to send you another mss that is a sort of statement of my position now.† It was written for a poet in Nicaragua, Pablo

*Erich Fromm, *Marx's Concept of Man.*
†"A Letter to Pablo Antonio Cuadra concerning Giants."

Antonio Cuadra, who by the way is running a magazine. I told him you might have something for him.

Did you say you might be coming this way in the fall? Do let us know if you can possibly make it to the Abbey. I am busy the first weekend in November and the first weekend in December, also somewhat busy around October 24, 25. Any other time is fine. I hope you will come this way.

> God bless you always,
> Affectionately in Christ
> Tom

I like the "Elegy" again in *Encounter*.* It says a lot.

※

5. X. 1961

Dear Merton,

My trip did not materialize, perhaps because of a routine or a feeling that there are many things to be done. It is like those canoe trips in my adolescence: before one was ready to go, one had to do that, and this. I have in my drawer a letter to you I did not send. But let's start by works. During my stay in Berkeley I wrote a certain number of pure, I hope, poems. You do not know my poems at all. A friend

---

*Zbigniew Herbert, "Elegy for Fortinbras," translated by Milosz, in *Encounter* 17:2 (August 1961).

of mine in Paris has translated some (they are short) into
French. I choose one by random:

Si je devais représenter ce qu'est pour moi le monde
je prendrais une marmotte ou une taupe ou un hérisson
je le placerais le soir dans un fauteuil de théâtre
et l'oreille collée contre son museau humide
j'écouterais ce qu'il dit des feux des réflecteurs
des sons de la musique, des mouvements du ballet.*

I thank you for *Wisdom of the Desert*, your dialogue with
Zen which I am reading and your poems on Hemingway,
on Auschwitz. The poem on Hemingway I like much.
Auschwitz—it comes like a voice from another planet, I
look at it through so many poems written in Polish and
unknown to the West.

There is that study on Brzozowski I am finishing. A very
important writer, died in 1911 at 32. Paid the price for
entering the forbidden domains: Historicité, Hegelianism,
Christianity. Do you know a book by Gaston Fessard S.J.
De l'historicité: Recherches Philosophiques? And Georges Cot-

---

*[If I had to tell what the world is for me / I would take a hamster or a hedgehog
or a mole / and place him in a theater seat one evening / and, bringing my ear close
to his humid snout, / would listen to what he says about the spotlights, / sounds of
the music, and movements of the dance.] From Milosz's poem "Throughout Our
Lands," in *King Popiel and Other Poems*, 1962, translated by Milosz and Peter Dale
Scott, in *Collected Poems*, 1988, p. 148. The poem was written in Berkeley in 1961.

tier *L'athéisme du jeune Marx: ses origines Hégeliennes*? In any case, to finish that study on Brzozowski, type it and send it away. It is interrupted all the time by my classes. Problem of teaching: my ambition of being good in that, not boring, and also I am sometimes panicky for another reason: how to convey what I feel in a dark, groping way—which can be conveyed only though a precision of writing and which has to be lost in speech—in speech I am ten times more loose and lacking precision. Besides, I have to present a certain conventional material, elementary things, historical events, writers, their biographies etc.

Then, as to Berkeley, my attitude, as I define it, of a catastrophist* emeritus. Pourvu que ça dure. A curiosity: how long can it last? Also a feeling that I don't make any use of my knowledge or rather experience of disasters, that I adapt myself perfectly to the American normality, with trumpets of doom blowing only in my dreams—and refused. Yet I could not write anything directly related to my feeling of precarity of everything. (Perhaps there is no such word in English—it comes from "précaire"). My poetry is serene.

I like my routine here. And one would like to have time, years, up to the end, and always your work will be interrupted in the middle of a phrase: God! Already? I have no time, let me finish this phrase, just nothing but this phrase.

---

*In 1931 Milosz founded a literary group called Zagary and their work was later termed "catastrophist" by critics because of its pessimistic and apocalyptic vision.

What to do with one's Christianity? Why do I consider myself a Christian? Traditions, their pressure? But I feel strongly, as a poet, that all is futility except our striving towards Being. In spite of all my hatred of the Thomists (usually totalitarians; a vengeance of time for their being inheritors of that crazy St. Dominic; what saved the Church from Eastern elements, from gnosis, taking shape via Bulgarian Bogomils in the Albigenses, is an indelible stigma of blood at the same time), in spite of that, I know that the only subject for a philosopher and for a poet is the verb "to be".

But all that noise of the world. And Catholicism taking the shape—always—of a political declaration. You know, in Poland the best intelligentsia is atheistic or agnostic, or in rare cases crypto-Catholic: not because of persecutions. A simplified image shows: the camp of darkness (the Communists), the camp of light (the Church, the Cardinal etc.). Yet the reality is more complicated. Divisions do not date from 1945 etc—they are of the XIX c. When peasants sometimes prayed to a picture of Leda with a swan, taking her for a saint. There is a tradition in Poland of a liberal, anticlerical intelligentsia—it is and it will be a motor of revolts. The Church is stained by its connivance with a frozen order, with conservatism, landowners' mentality. This is true not only for Poland. As a result, Poland in the XXth c. has had no Catholic writers. To say I am a Catholic is equivalent of a political declaration. And of course to say: I am a progressive Catholic is impossible over there, is ridiculous, is to bow to the expectations of the government. My friends of *Znak* are victims of great contradictions.

Et si Pascal n'a pas été sauvé
et ces mains étroites où l'on a placé une croix
c'est bien lui, comme une hirondelle morte,
dans la poussière, sous le bourdonnement des mouches
    bleues?*

Dear Merton, I cannot say I found my place in that world of contingencies. I cannot proclaim myself a Catholic, if I do not know whether I am one. And even if I knew, there are contingencies of a special Polish situation. Perhaps Wyszynski in the long run is doing a good job. But we are in a crisscrossing battle. There are more than two sides. How many people in the world today are crypto-religious?? How many stand in various Newman Halls like here with a "bouche bée"? At the sight of gymnastics called a Holy Mass?

I lump too many things together. I do not pretend to be orderly. You know, I think of writing on Swedenborg, who is undoubtedly the father of all modern—symbolical and

*And what if Pascal had not been saved / and if those narrow hands in which we laid a cross / are all he is, entire, like a lifeless swallow / in the dust, under the buzz of the poisonous-blue flies? Part of "Throughout Our Lands," translated by Milosz and Scott, *Collected Poems*, 1988, p. 150.

metaphorical—poetry. Has anybody compared Swedenborg with the subterranean wanderings of Dante? Swedenborg still is considered nothing but a crank. Perhaps he was. No more than modern (since Poe and Baudelaire) poetry. It does not mean that I want to secularize him, limit him to phenomena explainable in terms of pure immanence.

Love
Czeslaw

※

Jan 18, 1962

Dear Czeslaw:

Your letters are the best, I think, and therefore the hardest to answer. Or rather not the hardest, but they are the ones for which one wants to reserve a good time. There is no good time. Everything is at sixes and sevens, unless one falls right through the floor of time into a kind of Zen dimension which is simple and which moves right along without reference to the nonsense of society and its institutions. Is such a thing possible?

Did that book of yours ever come out, I mean the French autobiographical one, that was supposed to be on the way two years ago? I was impatient then and still am. Your study of Brzozowski is in French or in English? I should have written to you long ago to ask if you have anything about nuclear war or catastrophe. I have been working on a collection of articles like this, including one by Lewis Mumford* who has been out there with you. Did you meet him? The collection† is by now put together and ready to print, articles against nuclear war, groping for peace in some way, lashing out at the stupidity of fanatics (always very easy, for we are ourselves fanatics on occasion). But it is better than it sounds and I think it will make some sense.

I can understand how you would find the Auschwitz poem like an exercise of some sort. What else can I do? Yet I think there is no harm in doing even that much. Meanwhile I am sending a couple of other things. Maybe you will like the "Song for the Death of Averroës." Do you suppose *Znak* would want one of the articles on peace? I send them anyway. There is a peace movement for such Catholics as are my close friends and think as I do, it is starting. The *Catholic Worker* is doing it, and I don't know what it will amount to. It makes sense as an act done for the sake of truth.

You don't know how well I understand what you say about not wanting to declare yourself a Catholic and wear the label, which is a political one more often than not, and

---

*Lewis Mumford (1895–1990), philosopher and historian of American art and architecture, author of *Sticks and Stones* (1924), *Art and Technics* (1952), *The City in History* (1961).

†*Breakthrough to Peace.*

which implies a certain social stand, and an attachment to certain institutional forms, with God far in the background. The only trouble is that this is not the meaning of the word Catholic. It is the complete evisceration of Catholicity, but one which has been expertly and thoroughly performed by Catholics themselves. Thus I feel a certain equanimity and even smugness at the thought of my own possible excommunication. I cannot be a Catholic unless it is made quite clear to the world that I am a Jew and a Moslem, unless I am execrated as a Buddhist and denounced for having undermined all that this comfortable and social Catholicism stands for: this lining up of cassocks, this regimenting of birettas. I throw my biretta in the river. (But I don't have one.)

Friends of mine in Nicaragua are running a fine little magazine and want something of yours for it. It is called *El Pez y la Serpiente* and is mostly full of Central American poetry and art. But they want all kinds of things from everywhere. Why not send one of your poems? The one about the marmot is certainly very much their style. The editor is the one whose poems I translated in the offprint that is with the Suzuki stuff. Pablo Antonio Cuadra. I will send you an open letter I wrote with a certain amount of rage and fervor, addressed to him, it is appearing in lots of places and is probably too hot for Poland or I would offer it to *Znak*. I will send you the version appearing in England, in February.

The way to reach Cuadra is simple: address him at La Prensa, Managua, Nicaragua. I can easily get the Fessard book, I have heard of it.

Your letter sounds good and you sound contented with your catastrophisme. I think we have about five years in which to finish that phrase, and before that to become detached from finishing that phrase. This I really must begin, for my own part. God bless you, and much friendship in Christ

Tom Merton

Dear Merton:

Just a few words to thank you for your letter and materials. "Song for the Death of Averroës"—of great beauty. I am completely puzzled by your papers on duties of a Christian and on war. Perhaps I am wrong. My reaction is emotional: no. Reasons: 1) My deep scepticism as to moral action which seems to me Utopian. 2) My distrust of any peace movements, a distrust shared probably by all the Poles, as we experienced to what use various peace movements served (the slogan *mourir pour Danzig* in 1939, the peace movement of Stalin, which started in 1948 with a congress in Poland). 3) Noble-sounding words turning around the obvious, because nobody would deny that atomic war is one of the greatest evils.

I have no right to have any opinions on politics in this country as I am not even a resident but a guest. Yet it seems to me that a great danger here is *exasperation* which pushes many people to the right. Any peace action should take into account its probable effects and not only a moral duty. It is possible that every peace manifesto for every 1 person converted throws 5 persons to the extreme right, by a reaction against "defeatism." What would be more important is action through the Roman Church, if possible, in order to warn people against easy or apparently easy solutions offered by various shades of the new right and warn the Catholics against my association with such well-looking patriotic societies. I am not contented with my catastrophism. Is it catastrophism? Perhaps one can live through it only once in one's life—I did, 1933–1939, and am retired. I do not think of war and peace. Finished my study on Brzozowski, I speak there of affinities between him and Teilhard de Chardin, in a new edition of Boris Pasternak's collected works, in Russian (University of Michigan). I discovered in the preface that Pasternak when asked what Western writer he liked especially answered: Teilhard de Chardin. The study on Brzozowski appears in Paris, in Polish, here only a fragment in English in "Slavic Studies" of our university.* My "autobiographical" books appeared in German, Knopf bought it here but it will take time, *The Twentieth Century* (autumn 1961) dedicated to the subject "The Gods." Julian Huxley surpassed himself in idiocy, his credo—what children in communist countries learn in primary schools, so they are impregnated later against such clerics of pure scientism. He takes it seriously. Perhaps the hope for religion is *in Marxist education*, literal empiricism is, I feel, more deadly.

I saw of late Antoninus. I like him. Did you see a book by a young Protestant theologian Gabriel Vahanian, *The Death of God*? Perhaps you should write on it.

I started a new book, one of a blind urge and with a hope I could be useful to some people if I succeed in writing it. But only gropings for the moment.

With love,
Czeslaw Milosz

*Milosz, "A Controversial Polish Writer: Stanislaw Brzozowski," *California Slavic Studies* 2:1963, pp. 53–95. See also Milosz's "A One-Man Army: Stanislaw Brzozowski," in *Emperor of the Earth: Modes of Eccentric Vision*, 1977.

Dear, dear Merton,

I am sad as I have been thinking these last times that perhaps I offended you, that I should not have used in a hurry so harsh words speaking of your writings for peace. You know I am absolutely without any competence in that matter. All I can do is to present my subjective attitude. I got so used to treat any talk on peace as a part of the ritual in the Soviet bloc, as a smokescreen spread by officialdom at celebrations, meetings etc. that my reaction is just a reflex, an emotional outburst. Here I avoid any people who take part in a pacifist propaganda, not only because of my experiences in Poland, also because of my experiences in France.

It does not mean that I treat lightly the message of the Pope on peace. Neither that I am for armaments ad infinitum. Yet some fashions, some mores tying together intellectual groups at a given moment do not incline me to admiration. They are probably a result of restlessness, of vagueness, of an urge to do something even if nobody knows what exactly should be done.

Accuse me of pride, you will be right. Whatever reasons, I simply cannot find in myself a sufficient temperature of excitement. Moreover I have constantly before my eyes a professor here who is the milk of human kindness, serving all the good causes, among them the pacifist cause, out of unlimited love for humankind, yet he is a perfect fool, maneuvered from behind the scene by a few really clever individuals.

As I say, I am not competent. The more one lives in America, the more everything seems complicated, I mean here, groups and tendencies. Yet I ask myself why you feel such a itch for activity? Is that so that you are unsatisfied with your having plunged too deep into contemplation and now you wish to compensate through growing another wing, so to say? And peace provides you with the only link with American young intellectuals outside? Yet activity to which you are called is perhaps different? Should you become a belated rebel, out of solidarity with rebels without cause? Now, when there is such a chaos in the world of arts and letters, the most sane, intelligent (and of the best literary style) are works of French theologians. They perform an important and lasting task. We are groping—and I say it based upon what young Catholics in Poland write—towards completely new images permitting perhaps to grasp religion again as a personal vision. I do not invite you to write theological treatises but much can be accomplished, it seems to me, through literary criticism for instance.

I cannot give you advice, it would sound ridiculous. I just

describe my thoughts on you these last times, if they are wrong do not pay to them any attention.

Love

Czeslaw Milosz

❋

Dear Merton,

I add. The question of peace movements is important here, in view of a violent controversy around the Christian Anti-Communist Crusade active now in the San Francisco Bay area. If I said "noble-sounding" words, you should not feel wounded, since you are a poet and you know that our feelings and our strategy in words are two different things.

Karl Jaspers a few years ago published a treatise on atomic war.* Perhaps his book was not publicized because his attitude, as always, is unpopular. He makes many distinctions and he does not refer to just or unjust wars, but says there are situations when death should be chosen, if the alternative is slavery.

I have read the papal message on peace. To apply it is very difficult. What I am rather against† is a tenet accepted

---

* The Atom Bomb and the Future of Man, translated by E. B. Ashton.
† Not in the papal message, of course. [Milosz's note]

openly or surmised that life is the supreme value. Perhaps everybody believes it, yet only a part of him believes it, another is ashamed to agree. Certain types of peace propaganda play upon the first part, and even if they start from other premises, in consequence make the first part legitimate.

As to efficacity of calls for peace, picketing etc., they probably rather increase the danger, as I said, 1) by exasperation and polarisation of opinion into two hostile camps, which is a boon for right radicals; 2) by a possible miscalculation over there, in the Kremlin, a possibility of making one step too far in the blackmail.

In placing both camps on the same level, one is guilty of injustice, as of the two not the West is pushing and probing for new ways of expansion. By whitening our side one is guilty of self-righteousness. But by a reaction against it, one puts both sides on the same level, which is wrong.

Hiroshima was a crime. But it left me in 1945 completely indifferent and, should I be ashamed, it touches me today to the same extent as cataclysms of nature or hundreds of thousands of those who die at this moment of cancer in various countries. The number of people who died in tortures in Auschwitz alone equals the whole population of Switzerland, while the Russians deported from Poland in 1939–1941 1.500.000. Neither Auschwitz nor Russian slave labor camps were feature of the war but of political systems. For that reason I have never met anybody in Poland who would condemn mass bombardment of German cities. Some people lost there their relatives and friends but no doubt. To what extent those bombardments were necessary or inevitable, I do not know, this is not a question which can be solved easily.*

I have heard of young Americans who go to Poland and behave there foolishly. They are so much for peace, against American imperialism, for Cuba etc. that they make themselves ridiculous. It does not mean that anybody in Poland longs for war. No, but there is a realism and a certain toughness, they understand mechanisms of politics better.

I have read several clandestine works from Russia (they are not available in English). All are concerned with moral degradation of average men and women.

Did you read Abram Tertz's *On Socialist Realism*?† A work written in the Soviet Union, my preface, the publisher (Pantheon Books) did not send me even one copy, so I cannot send.

With love

Czeslaw

---

*Notice that war cannot be discussed *per se*. In the past, yes, not in the XXth c. [Milosz's note]

†Abram Tertz, *On Socialist Realism*, translated by G. Dennis. Introduction by Czeslaw Milosz.

Dear Czeslaw:

There are few people whose advice I respect as much as I do yours, and whatever you say I take seriously. Hence I do not feel at all disturbed or unsettled by what you say concerning my articles about peace, because I can see the wisdom of your statements and I agree with them to a great extent.

This is one of those phases one goes through. I certainly do not consider myself permanently dedicated to a crusade for peace and I am beginning to see the uselessness and absurdity of getting too involved in a "peace movement". The chief reason why I have spoken out was that I felt I owed it to my conscience to do so. There are certain things that have to be clearly stated. I had in mind particularly the danger arising from the fact that some of the most belligerent people in this country are Christians, on the one hand fundamentalist Protestants and on the other certain Catholics. They both tend to appeal to the bomb to do a "holy" work of destruction in the name of Christ and Christian truth. This is completely intolerable and the truth has to be stated. I cannot in conscience remain indifferent. Perhaps this sounds priggish, and perhaps I am yielding to subtle temptations to self-righteousness. Perhaps too there is a great deal of bourgeois self-justification in all this. Perhaps I am just trying to make myself feel that I am still in continuous contact with the tradition of my fathers, in English history, fighting for rights and truth and so on. And so on. In other words there is a large element of myth in it all. And yet one cannot know everything and analyze everything. It seems that there may be some point in saying what I have said, and so I have said it.

You are right about the temptation to get lined up with rebels without a cause. There is something attractive and comforting about the young kids that are going off into non-violent resistance with the same kind of enthusiasm I used to have myself in the thirties for left-wing action. But this too may be a great illusion. I trust your experience.

As far as I am concerned I have just about said what I have to say. I have written four or five articles, which are gradually getting published, hailed, attacked, and causing a small stir. I may revise them all and put them together into a small book. One publisher wants such a book badly and has made an enormous offer for it. Etc. I am not going to rush into this, however.

I think that I will have to remain available to speak up from time to time about the issue in moments of critical decision, or perhaps not.

In a word I have many doubts myself about all this. It seems to be largely self-deception. Yet to the best of my ability to judge, I feel that what I have done so far was necessary. Perhaps it was not done well. Perhaps it was naive. Undoubtedly I have not said the last word, nor has all that I have said been perfectly objective and well balanced. The fact that some Catholics are now angry with me is the least of my worries. I think too one of the articles may even have disturbed the President, and I don't want to be unfair to him. I have never aimed anything I said directly at any one person or small group.

Apart from that, however, I do think that the way people are going in this country there is growing evidence that a nuclear war is inevitable. Unless something unforeseen comes in to alter the whole picture.

I think too that you are right to some extent about the literary criticism, but that too involves a somewhat inordinate and impertinent activity. I think what I would most like to do and intend to do when I get the time is to translate some Latin American poetry with notes on the authors and the poems. Also I am trying to get time to work on the Chinese classical philosophy.

Here is a piece you might like, on Wisdom, Sophia. It says what is closest to my own heart. I enclose a poem also, in fact two poems. I do not think either of these was sent to you.

Meanwhile, I enjoy the spring rains (and there have been a lot of them) and am getting ready to do my usual planting of tree seedlings for reforestation.

Keep well, and thanks for all your advice and for your understanding. I repeat that I value both. God bless you always,

> Very cordially in Christ
> Tom.

※

Czeslaw Milosz   May 18, 1963
978 Grizzly Peak Blvd.
Berkeley 8, California

Dear Merton,

I don't know how to start the letter—so long time and yet so swift passage of time. So ad rem. Last year, I published in the monthly *Kultura* my translation of "Elegy for Hemingway". My promise to send you Polish poems in my translation into English has been gnawing at my conscience but I was waiting until more poems would be ready. Yet my work on that slowed down because of teaching, studying etc. also because it is very difficult to find students competent enough to correct my English. I did not make any steps, either, to have those poems published, except that I have sent a bunch of them, some time ago, to James Laughlin, asking him to read them and to pass the bunch to you. Have you heard from him?

Of late I had a reading of those poems at the Holy Names College for girls in Oakland; excellent response of nuns, a true contact.

I spent the last year on turning around Robinson Jeffers. This may surprise you. In any case any serious preoccupation with Jeffers surprises many today. I believe the low ebb is something temporary for he was in a way a gigantic figure. I treat him comparatively so to say, i.e. meditating on Polish, Russian, French and American poetry of today and of the future. Very much noise and blubbering and we do not see clearly, for me emerging figures of a monumental achievement are Cavafy, Jeffers. Anything which turns against reducing poetry to a kind of an Indian tribe slowly dying out in a reservation of "language lyrique". The reason I am attracted by Jeffers is probably the same I am attracted by you. Not poetry "per se" but an effort to communicate a vision of the universe. Jeffers, after all, was writing *De Natura Rerum.* By the way, Simone Weil considered Lucretius the only Roman poet, redeeming, to some extent, Roman (worthless) literature. A similar view in our poet of the 1st half of the XIX c, Mickiewicz. Perhaps Jeffers illustrates "belatedness" common to American and Russian literature when compared with

Western Europe. After Nietzsche, the courage to attack such problems waned in Europe. Of course, I recognize that long poems of Jeffers are failures. And I cannot agree with his Weltanschauung. But exactly the question why I cannot agree is a constant challenge. I have translated several of his poems.*

Poland. The whole vivifying intellectual turbulence canalized by the party into pettiness and looking for jobs. Catholics pay a heavy price of compromise, assuming their role, ordinary in Poland, of the political right, of a collaborating right, an opposition of His Majesty, with a special field assigned to them: patriotic hatred of Germans and defense of the Polish right to Oder-Neisse borders. As a result moral and political issues mixed up, blurred. A scourge of Polish Catholicism. This spring semester I have been giving a course on the Reformation and the Counter-Reformation in Poland, concentrating upon socinianism† (Poland was the country of socinianism in Europe).

America. My indignation, at the TV for instance, is over. Rather a feeling of sadness at the view of waste. Helplessness and contentment. For I am glad to be here and I like teach-

*Milosz has written several essays on Jeffers, most notably "Carmel," which appeared in *Visions from San Francisco Bay*, translated by Richard Lourie; and "Robinson Jeffers: An Attempt at Disclosure," in *Beginning with My Streets*, translated by Madeline G. Levine. One of Milosz's most memorable lyrics is "To Robinson Jeffers," which appears with the "Carmel" essay and in *Collected Poems*, 1988.

†Socinianism is an extreme form of Hellenized Christianity that denies Christ's divinity and provides rationalist explanations of sin and salvation.

ing. What an alibi! I catch myself on reluctance to add words to that monstrous pile of printed words. In Europe I was forced to write, just by financial circumstances. Some friends (snobbish) are deserting me because I do not keep my "fame" hot and "everybody will forget you". But I dislike fiction—whether to read it or to write it is equally boring, while I cannot say anything valid on communism and have always shunned the role of an "expert". I feel the whole problem is moving into a new dimension, if you prefer, by meditation on Jeffers one can perhaps touch that new dimension, too.

Poems, novels, films, plays exploiting alienation? Abominable complexity of neurotics. A trash can. I wonder whether my feelings are not exactly like those of a classicist confronted with ravings of romantics let us say in 1820–1830. Undoubtedly that "cultural criticism" is a smokescreen. Perhaps more vulgar, less sophisticated interpretation of human fate is more healthy. I doubt whether anybody would be able to convince me that Western Europe for instance is "back to the normal". If back to normal, then to the normal of the filthy "belle époque". Diamonds and hovels, a facade, my 10 years there, humiliations of a refugee intellectual, not very different from humiliations of a native intellectual, a buffoon of those who have money. So in order to earn honestly one's bread one goes to America.

In the second half of June I go with my family to Europe, I have my semi-sabbatical, so we would stay there until January. I am curious of my impressions, one goes constantly through such changes of mental climate. An abyss, images juxtaposed, from my childhood I remember scenes of World War I (Russian–German front, Polish–Soviet war 1920) and of the Russian revolution (in a little town on the Volga).

I went to confession on Easter and, as usual, rather bad results. I have a need of humility and contrition and I am grateful to God. Yet there is something wrong with the institution, how to improve it, I do not know. No absolution can erase the past and, besides, I have a feeling I am a liar— my guilt is shapeless, all-embracing, when I try to express it, I distort. And what to confess? I would be happy to know at least my sins, I do not know them, only at moments they appear in a flash and then disappear in a kind of magma. Not to speak of a priest's interests, in rubrics, in Law.

Only theology is important. This is the new dimension I gather under modern paraphernalia. Cravings of man will not be satisfied cheaply. Look at the Soviet Union. I know a case of a Soviet writer who when on a visit in the West bought a lot of books, nearly all of them on religious subjects. Yet we will not see men on the other side of that threshold they are approaching (if the species survives). It takes time. Some 20–30 years have to elapse after every revolution before people get disillusioned with ideology, then for 20–30 years they have to fall into traps of modern art serving as a substitute. Perhaps timing here is wrong but it takes time. Yet the present moment is interesting. And the present pope guessed much.

With love
Czeslaw

※

Nov 11, 1963

Dear Milosz:

I waited quite a while for Laughlin to send the Polish poets, and then when he sent them, having read them immediately with a great deal of pleasure, I let too much time go by, I got in a hospital and out again, and now I have forgotten all that I wanted to say about them. But in general I want to say this that they are poets I can read, and want to read, and agree with exactly. This they have in common for me with Latin American poets. I find it difficult to keep my mind on the poets of the US except one or two like William Carlos Williams, but your Polish poets fascinate me and I find myself in complete resonance with them their moods, their irony, their austerity, their simplicity. I feel that these are really honest men speaking to me and that there is no nonsense about their poetry: it is something to be received with complete simplicity.

I like Wat* very much (his Brueghel one is fine) but especially Zbigniew Herbert. This I think is some of the best poetry of our time, and it is about what happens, except to them, or what they imagine might be happening inside them. This is not enough.

Thanks for translating the "Elegy to Hemingway." I wonder if I could have a copy of that issue of *Kultura*, as there is someone who collects all my translations. I would appreciate it.

I am glad you have been working on Jeffers. I can see what would attract you in him, though I have not read him much. There is too much of him, and he is too grandiloquent for me in some ways. I have never been attracted to him much. But this is my fault and not his. Mark Van Doren† likes him and I like Van Doren (one of the rare poets here I can read). Nor have I ever got into Lucretius. Personally I like Horace and Virgil, and I think Virgil is an unquestionably great one. I have always loved the Georgics, and Horace's Odes.

---

*Alexander Wat (1900–67), futurist writer, author of *Lucifer Unemployed*. A selection of Wat's poems translated by Milosz and Leonard Nathan entitled *With the Skin* was published in 1990. His autobiography, *My Century: The Odyssey of a Polish Intellectual* (1977, English translation by Richard Lourie, 1988), was developed in taped conversations with Milosz in Berkeley.

†Mark Van Doren (1894–1972), poet, critic, and anthologist, and one of Merton's mentors at Columbia University. In addition to biographies of Thoreau, Shakespeare, and Hawthorne, Van Doren's books include *Spring Thunder and Other Poems* (1924), *The Mayfield Deer* (1941), *Spring Birth* (1953), *Morning Worship and Other Poems* (1960). His *Collected Poems* (1940) was awarded the Pulitzer Prize.

You talk about Polish Catholics: their right wing function etc. This is the disturbing thing. I think of the Viet Nam bunch, that was just cleaned up. One of them, Nhu,* had been a student of Mounier.† But he came along with strategic hamlets and fascist police and all the rest of it. Aggressive Catholicism, sure of itself, deeply involved in a power struggle, content to be purely anti-communist, gentle to everyone but those who need it, and harsh to them: etc. This is the sickening picture that should not be everywhere, but is. Yet the Pope is not like that, John XXIII was not. Perhaps the French Catholics, in part, are not.

As for TV I still haven't seen any, and am not disposed to be content with it if I do, but I can see that you cannot go on with perpetual indignation about it. And as for keeping your fame "hot,"—what for? Why do your friends object to the temperature of your fame? Perhaps because they are the kind of friends who collect famous friends. You do not have to warm them. I agree with you on your dislike of fiction and can't read most novels even when I try, but now I am well into an enormous one, Gironella's great, laconic (yet enormous) novel of the Spanish Civil War, *One Million*

*Ngo Dinh Diem (1901–63), president of the Republic of Vietnam (South Vietnam) from 1954 until his assassination, and a convert to Catholicism.

†Emmanuel Mounier (1905–50), Catholic philosopher and disciple of Bergson, Maritain, and Péguy who strongly opposed Marxism and Sartre.

*Dead.** I think it is something everyone should read, though it starts slow and has thousands of characters.

About confession: again I understand what you mean. It is a very institutional sort of thing, especially the "Easter duty" business. But how can one confess to an institution? And what kind of forgiveness is dispensed by an organization? One puts in his bid and gets his return slip. There has to be a deeper sense of union with people, a union that is ruptured by sin. If I confess a sin it should be because I feel that the sin has divided me from *you*, and has hurt you, or has hurt someone here, closer to me. Or it has hurt Christ in His Body. But the devotional nonsense that tries to cover up the institutional aspect of it with ideas that sin hurts Christ in Himself, now. Nonsense. It hurts Him only in His members, or with reference to them and our common union, with Him. The sins that are said to attack God directly, pride rebellion and so on, attack Him only *in myself.* They destroy His likeness in me, they cannot touch Him. Anyway the whole notion of sin is so corrupted by juridical considerations.

Still the piece I enclose is silly and not to be taken as having anything to say really about sin. Still, it has something to say about ideas of sin, and ideas which I think are wrong. But nevertheless they are quite real.

*J. M. Gironella, *One Million Dead,* translated by J. MacLean (Garden City: Doubleday, 1963).

It is always very good to hear from you. Please write, I want to have your news and I will try to be better about replying myself, instead of just getting sunk in a morass of letters that are easy to answer because they say nothing.

You should not plague yourself about the superficial aspect of your relation to the Church. The deeper is much more significant and you do not see it, neither does the "Church" of those who think they have their eye on everything that goes on in the world of "souls". The Church is fortunately a mystery that is beyond the reach of bureaucracy, though sometimes one is tempted to doubt it.

> With all blessings and affection in Christ
> Tom.

✳

August 31, 1964

Dear Merton,

I am supposed to be in Chicago around Sept. 10 and at last I see the occasion to fly to Louisville first. Possibly on Sept. 8 or 9. If you tell me that a visit at that time would not be an interference with your occupations. Of course I would be a burden as I wish to talk. Tell me frankly whether I should come.

> Yours loving
> Czeslaw

Dec. 19, 1964

Dear Milosz:

Just a word to wish you the blessings of the holy season and to say I have recently written to Anne Freedgood with a statement about the anthology.* I had her send me proofs as I wanted to read it at leisure, and I am more convinced than ever that it is excellent. Your notes are very helpful, and your own poems are by no means the least interesting in the book. I especially like the Ghetto one.† The whole book really gives an impression of life and direction. Poland is alive, poetically, and I find that the Polish poets are people with whom I can feel myself in the greatest and most spontaneous sympathy. They speak directly to me, and I respond to them much more than I do to the poets in the US, or France, perhaps even England (though I do like some of the young English poets a lot). I respond to these as much as I do to some of the Latin Americans. The very young ones are quite encouraging too. Some of the surrealist stuff is better and more real than anything else that has come out of that trend.

It was very good to have you here—how long ago?‡ Since

* *Postwar Polish Poetry*, edited by Czeslaw Milosz, 1965.
† "A Poor Christian Looks at the Ghetto," from *Rescue* (1945).
‡ Milosz had visited Merton in September.

then Bro Antoninus was here too, he is going about reading his poems, probably is back there by now, but no longer in Oakland. Back in the hills somewhere.

My new book is in print, with a lot of material on peace.* I will send you a copy if I can lay hands on an extra one. Meanwhile I enclose an article that might amuse you. Let it serve as my Christmas card. What is new with you? I hope you are well, and good luck to you in the New Year. God bless you.

Cordially always in Christ,
Tom Merton

※

December 31, 64/65

Dear Tom,

I write this on New Year's Eve which we spend traditionally at home, without any company, since that day of 1944/5 when I got drunk in quite inappropriate circumstances. Thus, to atone or to express our gratitude for not having been punished immediately after my stupid acts. Thanks for your letter: a good New Year gift, and for your essay which is very didactic, a sermon addressed to Ameri-

*Seeds of Destruction.

cans. I had some difficulty in applying it to my problems and I came to the conclusion that it applies to my literature, to my literary ambition.

1. I write less and less poetry and I am becoming a dreamer, i.e. I measure the distance between what I would like to write and what I could (I feel) write on the one hand and what I can write on the other, with the result that I write nothing. My nights are filled with ecstatic prayers, with joy—I know it can be just a trap but I cannot struggle against the evidence. I am well acquainted with the role of what is called "le rêve" abolishing any accomplishment but to my surprise I return to my adolescence, to toying with possibilities. Yet this is my pain also, my desire of being useful, interwoven with my personal literary ambition, push me toward doing something. In this time of universal negation and sneering should not one express admiration? But perhaps I do not deserve it, God has so many gifted people at his disposal. As you see "useful" and "useless" can take on some peculiar forms.

2. My son, Toni. A very irritating and often stupid adolescent but I am completely under his spell. My fears and my complexities, horror of inherited, my own, weaknesses seen suddenly as if in a mirror. Through him an insight into the very young America, perhaps not quite typical ("beats", culture of drugs and not culture of alcohol, Zen, philosophy)

but very important. Lazy, contemplative, bright, sarcastic, idealistic, weak, he discovers that sub-society of Berkeley which has in this country an equivalent only in Greenwich Village. Their crazy sessions of infinite discussions from which alcohol is absent. Crazy with Zen, admiring Aelred Graham's *Zen Catholicism,** his passion is history of religions, at the university where he is a freshman he takes a course in religions of Iran. But he does not go to church (discipline!). My younger son, Peter, goes with me to church. A quiet one, perhaps a true contemplative. I do not go to Communion. My upbringing, I do not feel worthy, and Confession is for me an obstacle, an absurdity. My sons never communicated. In France la prémière communion was just ridicule, I did not want to make atheists out of them. And I do not know how to proceed now. Long discussions with Toni on drugs (cleansing the gates of perception). I gave to him Baudelaire on hashish—Baudelaire was obsessed with passivity resulting from drugs, it was an offense to his stress on will, besides he saw a temptation of the Devil through the Ego feeling equal to God. Baudelaire deserves in my opinion our greatest respect, not Rimbaud. Except that Rimbaud was wise enough to reject his poetry. But it seems to me you should pay attention to drugs. They are quite an element in the life of the young generation.

*Aelred Graham, *Zen Catholicism: A Suggestion*, 1963.

3. The liturgical reform. Yes. But the mass in English a mistake. Think of millions who feel deprived of something, like myself: immigrants from Eastern Europe, Italians in Germany and France, Spaniards—workers all over Europe, Mexicans in this country. And the chasm between Latin America and the U.S. will be deeper. Why to "protestantise" the Church in those aspects which are the least valid? Why not leave the mass in Latin in those countries which are used to it (Asia, Africa are something else). If the mass should be in the vernacular now, when in Europe and Northern America literacy is a rule, then Latin in the epochs when the majority was illiterate was a monstrosity. Now they all have missals with parallel Latin—vernacular texts. Please, write on that subject.

4. Months of turmoil at our university. Nobody in America understands what those sit-ins and strikes are about. But the less they understand the more they are eager to sign petitions and manifestos in defense of oppressed students. Including telegrams from England, from Bertrand Russell. All those months, since October, I was more busy with innumerable meetings and committees than with teaching. Very exciting. But the truth is the proclaimed aims of the students have little to do with dynamics of the movement. It happened in Berkeley because: 1) Berkeley is, like Greenwich Village, a center of a sub-society of the young generation which rejects all the values of the society at large, takes "alienation" and

dehumanisation of "squares" for granted. What one should preach here is a bit of pity and compassion for "squares". 2) The university is too big, a Kafka-like maze of IBM machines, the pride of the administration. 3) The administration proved its stupidity in handling touchy issues. The mass of the students following the leaders found valid reasons to join the movement. Yet the name: Free Speech Movement is demagoguery. What they ask for is an official recognition, by a State university, of the right to organize on the campus illegal actions directed against the community at large, namely, sit-ins at those institutions which do not employ a sufficient number of Negroes. The administration grants them that right in petto, they press for an official proclamation. The gist of the question is not in those avowed aims. The movement produced excellent leaders, born tacticians (Mario Savio, Goldberg, Weissman) and is the first authentic Castroist movement in this country. Not in the sense they are followers of Castro (though among the leaders there are Castroists in that sense) but because of intrinsic patterns. I went along as far as I could because I am sympathetic to civil rights actions. At a given moment I bolted, I said no. A split within the faculty is a fact now. You mention in your essay the *Lord of the Flies*. This is exactly it, the birth of a ferocious community applying intimidation to those students and those professors who would not comply. I know these things by heart from Europe. There is a lot of fog around: ninety per cent of those who follow are in a fog—otherwise they would not follow. I take a very serious view. This is but the first stage of an all-American movement. Great energies of the young generation cannot turn round in a void. Oswald was an example of energies of negation went wild. My observation on professors who joined the movement: they are haters, either because their hatred of America (Moloch, dehumanization, business, machines, capitalism etc.) is genuine or because it is fashionable. Protestant, Jewish and Catholic "chaplains" (Newman Hall) backed, with some reservations, the movement, to flatter the students and to be on the band wagon. To look at it soberly, as at a revolution in the kindergarten (the tactics are on the scale of Venezuela, the pretexts are childish) is an offense. But, believe me, I am not on the side of senseless destruction and the very existence of our university is endangered. As to squares, managers, businessmen, I take a quite detached attitude, while many students and some professors would be able to send them to concentration camps. I wonder whether you, Tom, being on the side of the young American sub-society, should not think sometimes that they are human beings too, in spite of their benighted minds. What we had here, in Berkeley, was a sudden realization that the bourgeois bugaboo is in fact very weak, defenseless, just scared, as in Russia of 1917. There is no doubt we lived here through a revolution, on a minor scale but reproducing all the features of a major event, including a leader—Mario Savio—dictating his conditions. You would be amused, no doubt. Please consider that the existence of a very small state, a university, was at stake, as in case it is closed down the majority of professors would migrate. The crisis is not over. In a few days we expect new demands and new actions.

New Year's Eve is approaching so I interrupt my letter to join my family.

Je vous embrasse
Czeslaw

米

March 30, 1965

Dear Czeslaw:

Your good reflective letter of New Year's Eve was one that I appreciated very much. In fact I saved it to read in a fine wild part of the woods where I had the whole day free, and I have not forgotten it. In fact I think that we are getting to be remarkably alike in a lot of ways. Since I am now fifty, and just in general since the past few months, I am very much revising my perspectives, my relationship to the younger generation. Your own thoughts about your sons were relevant to me in many ways too, though of course I am quite remote from their problems, and yet involved in them. The novices here of course do not have the same kind of problem, most of them never having been in any sense intellectuals. Their problems are relatively simple. I have still only the vaguest understanding of the Berkeley trouble, but everything I see about it shows that it is a symptomatic and sensitive area. But from this I am really remote, I am afraid. I understand your reservations about it though, and I understand exactly what you say about the need of compassion for squares, though I must confess that I am not always perfectly sensitive to that need.

For instance: I am happy that nuns appeared in the march at Selma, I met a priest who was there and he is a fine guy, it is all right etc. But the trouble is that it is so simple that it is already ambiguous the moment it happens. This is the thing that I am up against at the moment, in my innocence of real politics: the fact that fine, simple upright intentions, which cry out for action, become, the moment they are put into effect, ambiguous, sinister, but in a way that nobody seems to notice. Right away the ambiguities become an institution, a pattern for future actions which are more and more sinister, or rather which bog down in futilities. Wait and see. Out of it all comes murder, corruption, lying . . . I am not laying this on the poor sisters. But the fact of the South that nobody seems to pay any attention to at the moment is that nothing is being done for the sickest and most morally impoverished of them all, Southern whites. Their stupidity and ferocity are, on the contrary, simply being driven to the extreme: of course they invite it. It would be too good not to let them ruin themselves and make fools of themselves (Wallace) but in the end our blissful charity will make perfect Nazis of them. They are that already, without any of the skill of the German types.

Thus I find myself in a position where I do not identify myself with groups and I am not going to sign petitions. It would be quite absurd and most ambiguous to get myself drawn into a movement of one sort or another, and I think the monastic life is a life of liberation from movements. This is of course in many ways reprehensible and open to criticism, and it has immense disadvantages. But there you are.

Thus you see that I am not identified with the young American sub-society. I give them my sympathy, but like you I stop at the business of hating for hating's sake what is so transparently easily hated. I see, as you do, the zeal that would end with them putting the squares in camps, except that perhaps the squares will turn out smarter and put *them* in camps. Precisely the point is to be one of those for whom there can be no such solutions even implicitly.

As for the new liturgy: there are people around I suppose who would be ready to assassinate, morally, anyone who admitted that he did not like English in the liturgy. I am not saying I like it or don't like it. We have some of the readings in English in the High Mass, and that is ok except the translations are terribly trite. But when I find monks wanting to throw out Latin altogether I hesitate. After all, our Latin liturgy is pretty good and very solid. It may not be exciting but it stands firm and holds up for year after year, and the chant is, as far as I am concerned, inexhaustibly good. I defy them to replace that with anything one tenth as good.

As to being in the know about dope in the spiritual life: I have made a couple of attempts to get information, but it was singularly uninformative. I would not be able to experiment with the stuff myself and would not want to, so in the end there is another area where I have nothing left but yawns. And I suppose that means another bond with the youth of the day has slipped.

And as to Zen, well, it might just turn out that my Zen had nothing to do with theirs, I don't know.

Thus your thoughtful letter has helped me to admit that I am not all that attached to the younger generation. All I know is that I sympathize with them and am open to them, but living in the woods as I do more and more, how can I pretend that I really know them? I have come around a corner, as you have, and I simply feel that there is so much of significance simply in my own living and doing or not doing such work as I do or don't do, that there is no further reason to imagine having an identity that is made up of relationship with new movements.

Still, it is true I do write for pacifist publications, and I send you a review of a book about Simone Weil I did recently.*

God bless you always. I have the book and it is handsomely done, and I like it as well and better than ever.

Cordially always in the Lord,
Tom.

※

Jan 5, 1968

Dear Czeslaw:

It is a long time since I have heard from you. In fact three years ago to the day I remember enjoying your last letter which I took with me for a full day out in the wilds across the valley here.

I hope you are still to be found at the same address. What I want to ask is this: can you send me a few translations of young Polishpoets for a little magazine† I am starting? The

---

*Merton reviewed Jacques Cabaud's *Simone Weil, Fellowship in Love* in *Peace News*. Reprinted as "Pacifism and Resistance" in Thomas Merton's *Faith and Violence: Christian Teaching and Christian Thought*.
†*Monks Pond.*

magazine will be free, literary and will also include texts from Asian religions and other interesting areas. I would love to have something Eastern European, for example a bit of your own reminiscences if available in English, or anything of yours and anything from the Polishpoets. Why I keep spelling that as one word is a mystery to me. . . .

How have you been? Let us hear some news of you! Hope you are well. My very best wishes to you and Happy New Year.

With all blessings,
Tom Merton

✺

15/I/68

Dear Tom:

I have lived through quite turbulent two years, very emotional. Also long stays in France. In March of this year I attended a conference of Polish poets and translators of Polish poetry, in Paris, a very unofficial affair looked upon with uneasiness by the Warsaw government. In September World Poetry Conference in Montreal, a rather pompous and useless event, except for fun we had visiting the expo with Adam Wazyk, a poet from Warsaw whom I like. During the time of my silence I wrote (dictated) an enormous volume in English—A history of Polish literature*, since the Xth c. till today, 880 pages, perhaps an idiotic exploit or an exercise in patience, which will blur even more my "public image"—nobody will know any more whether I am the author of *The Captive Mind*, a poet, a translator or a scholar. It is going to be published by Macmillan. But also I have made progress in poetry, I hope I hit something and am trying to write an essay on the subject, roughly, of "California and I" or "The Twentieth Century and I".†

Of course, I want to contribute to your magazine. I do not care for magazines edited by abstract figures. Can you say anything about the title, contents, deadlines? As to young Polishpoets I have to say no. I feel I did my share and proved my civic spirit by serving them as a translator but the situation changed. Polish literature has always moved forward by short-lived spurts, there are 50.000 poets in Poland now but nobody is first-rate, Poland now is again a bog like under Stalinism, except that instead of the doctrine you have a kind of a vanguard and western masturbation. The best people go abroad and stay there for years, just not to be in the bog. The Party is busy now with chasing down Jews suspected of sympathies for Israel etc. Plenty of half-émigrés like Herbert who has been living in France

* *The History of Polish Literature*, 1969.

†This became *Visions from San Francisco Bay*, first published in Polish in Paris in 1969.

these years or new émigrés. If I can send you something this would be a few of my poems in translation.

The Church. I have had letters from a close friend of mine, Turowicz, the editor of the *Everybody's Weekly* (*Tygodnik Powszechny*) in Cracow, from Rome, where he presided over a lay committee or something of the sort. I told him in my letters my suspicions, that perhaps John XXIII was an Antichrist—it is obvious that the Antichrist after so many centuries of experiences could not appear under a *less* clever disguise. I advised Turowicz to start a new heresy in Poland, consisting in an exact reversal of the existing trends, namely, to cling to Latin and to the traditional liturgy and to drop any concerns with sex, the pill etc. But no heresy will come from Poland. Maybe I am wrong but it seems to me the Roman Church aspires now to the situation of Protestantism, which cannot be worse. My prediction—and I wish I were wrong—is that the number of homeless religious minds will be rapidly increasing.

love
Czeslaw

❋

Dear Thomas:

I know I wounded you by my last letter. Forgive me. Forgive my stupid and cruel jokes. I am afraid, however, of a misunderstanding. I am not on the side of Catholic conservatives. I am not one of those who shout: "you go too far!" I am an outsider and have no right whatsoever to quarrel about what the Church should do. All I know is that a church building in America is now at last what it aspired to be for a long time: a place of genuinely American, Boy-Scoutish cheerfulness. Untainted by abominable souvenirs of Latin chants and of medieval *danses macabres*. I am not cheerful and I am not for a national togetherness, be it American, Mexican, or Polish. Whether the rotten wood should be hidden under a layer of varnish or revealed as it is, remains to be seen. The second solution is probably better.

I suffer because of Vietnam, of the ghettos, of Poland, of my inability to express what should be expressed. I have not much interest in the Church. I admired Pope John XXIII as a good man.

Love
Czeslaw

Dear Czeslaw:

Let me reassure you. There was absolutely nothing wounding in your letter. Anything you may be tempted to think about the Church, I think myself, and much more so as I am in constant contact with all of it. The boy scout atmosphere, the puerile optimism about the "secular city" and all the pathetic maneuvers to be accepted by the "world"—I see all this and much more. And I also get it from the other side. Conservative Catholics in Louisville are burning my books because I am opposed to the Viet Nam war. The whole thing is ridiculous. I do think however that some of the young priests have a pathetic honesty and sincerity which is very moving. Beyond that, I have nothing to say. And I have a thick skin. You can say absolutely nothing about the Church that can shock me. If I stay with the Church it is out of a disillusioned love, and with a realization that I myself could not be happy outside, though I have no guarantee of being happy inside either. In effect, my "happiness" does not depend on any institution or any establishment. As for you, you are part of my "Church" of friends who are in many ways more important to me than the institution.

So don't worry about your letter, or anything else of the sort.

I have been meaning to send you a copy of my magazine,

which, as you will see, is concerned with nonorthodoxies, whether poetic or religious. If you can think of anything that would fit into it, please send me something.

Take care of yourself. Peace and joy.

My very best,

※

July 1 1968

Dear Czeslaw

I'm fighting my way through another issue* of my magazine, and am consoled by the quality of so much good stuff. I want to use your Sentences.† May I please?

Thanks and best wishes,
Tom Merton

※

*_Monks Pond_, Fall, 1968.
    †A poem by Milosz, in _Bobo's Metamorphosis_, 1965. It appears in _Collected Poems_, 1988.

Monks Pond   July 29 1968
Trappist, Kentucky 40073

Dear Czeslaw:

The Penguin selection of Herbert is splendid.* A very
fine book. I keep being impressed by his work. Was he in
this country this spring? I seem to have heard something of
it. I'd have liked to meet him.

Anyway: I'd like to reprint a group of seven or eight of
the little prose poems that are around pp. 63ff. This will be
in my fourth and last issue of *MPond.* I could also perhaps
do a short note on ZH. However, if you also have one or
two unpublished translations of Herbert that you could
spare—that would be good, and would save me from just a
section of reprints. I don't like to reprint anything that has
been done in this country, and Penguin really is American
as well as English. But Herbert is so fine.

I might be in California in October—whizzing through
SF very briefly. I don't like to stay in any city more than a
few hours. Are you going to be around? Could we get together in a SF restaurant for lunch? (I don't want to come
to Berkeley particularly, it's off my route*. I'm heading up

*Zbigniew Herbert, *Selected Poems,* translated by Czeslaw Milosz and Peter Dale
Scott, 1968.
*But I can if necessary.[Merton's note]

the coast to our nuns near Eureka) Let me know and perhaps we can arrange something.

Best always,
Tom

Please let me know about permission to use the bits from Penguin.

※

Darjeeling   Nov 21 [1968]

Dear Czeslaw,
I have been in India about a month & have met quite a few interesting people. Seen monasteries, temples, lamas, paintings, jungles—not to mention the arch-city of Calcutta. Quite an experience. I will be going on soon to Ceylon & Indonesia. Hope you are both well. It was good to see you in SF.

Best,
Tom Merton